The Commodity Boot Camp, Ltd.SM
BASIC TRAINING MANUAL

William I. Greenspan, Author
Ross J. Greenspan, Editor

Commodity Boot Camp, Ltd.SM

Table of Contents

1 INTRODUCTION TO FUTURES

Futures markets provide a meeting place for buyers and sellers. For every transaction, there has to be a buyer and seller. The buyer is said to have a long position while the seller is said to have a short position. Each transaction creates 1 contract of trading volume.

Forward contracts are contracts initiated at one point in time and concluded at a subsequent time. A futures contract is a form of a forward contract but with some special features. Futures contracts trade on organized exchanges in specific trading locations called pits and during specified trading hours. Futures contracts have standardized contract terms. Buyers and sellers only negotiate on price. Futures exchanges have clearinghouses to guarantee all futures contract. Creditworthiness of the counterparties is not an issue in futures trading. Futures trading is settled daily. All profits and losses are realized at the end of each trading day. Futures trades require a performance bond to initiate a trade. Futures markets are highly regulated by government and industry bodies.

There are 2 types of traders. The first is a hedger. Hedgers have exposure in the cash market and want to trade away their risk. The other type of trader, the speculator, wants to trade the risk for potential profit.

There are 2 types of brokers. The first is an account executive for a brokerage firm. The account executive works with customers and is their interface to the trading floor. The floor broker is a broker on the trading floor who executes orders for customers.

Futures contracts are settled daily. Traders realize any gains or losses in their accounts as of the settlement price daily. The trader may be required to post additional money to continue to hold his position. If he does not deposit additional money, his position will be liquidated at the earliest opportunity.

Futures exchanges have associated clearinghouses. The clearinghouse guarantees that all traders will honor their contracts. The clearinghouse is the counterparty to all transactions.

There are 3 ways to close a futures contract. The first is to take delivery or settle the contract in cash. The most common is the offsetting or reversing trade where a trader brings his net position to 0 for a particular contract. The last and least common is the exchange for physicals trade.

There are 4 types of futures contracts. There are futures on foreign currencies, interest earning assets, indexes, and physical commodities.

Futures markets provide price discovery and hedging. Price discovery allows society to allocate resources in the present for capital outlays in the future. Hedging allows those who do not want to trade risk a way to shift the risk elsewhere.

Cash and futures markets are linked. Futures prices reflect the cash price carried forward to the contract's expiration date. The future's price reflects the cash price plus the cost of carry. The cost of carry includes interest expenses plus storage, insurance, and transportation costs if applicable. In normal markets, futures prices will be greater than cash prices.

Futures markets are regulated by the Commodity Futures Trading Commission (CFTC), the National Futures Association (NFA), and the exchanges. The NFA screens and tests potential members of the industry. It tests their industry knowledge and ethical fitness. It also establishes capital trading requirements and customers records. The CFTC approves new contracts, trading rules, etc. The exchanges impose minimum margin requirements.

TYPES OF ORDERS

Limit Order

A limit order is when a floor broker is ordered to bid the market up to, or offer the market down to a specific price. It is understood that if he can execute the order at a better price, he will do so. A limit order directs the floor broker to buy or sell the designated contracts at the stipulated price or better. Limit buy orders are usually entered below the prevailing market price and sell limits above it. An exception is when you are willing to pay the market price but want to protect yourself against any runaway price movement. A limit order would then be placed slightly above (maybe 3 ticks) the last price to assure a buy in a rising market or just below, to get a sale off in a falling market. If the market remains unchanged while the order finds its way to the pit, you might receive a better price; but you are allowing a little room to maneuver, in case the market begins to move. The risk of using a limit order, rather than a market order, is that should the market move through your price before the order can be executed, you must sit and watch the market go in your direction. Traders who enter market orders, therefore, have the assurance that their orders will be executed, but they have little control over price. If you use limit orders, you retain control over price but you run the risk' of missing the market. All in all, a trader is better off using a limit order. It can always be revised.

Market Order

The basic order is the market order. This is the most common type of order. It tells the floor broker to buy or sell a specific amount of contracts of a given delivery month at the prevailing price when the order hits the pit. The floor broker will receive the order in the pit and cry out "market." The local traders and other floor brokers will announce the bid and offer in the "open outcry" fashion and the order will be executed. A sell order will be sold to the highest bid and a buy order will be bought by the lowest offer. Futures price can move with amazing speed during busy market sessions. The price that is being quoted over the phone is not available seconds later and when you do place a market order, you will sometimes find that the order was executed at a price far different than the price quoted over the phone or seen on your quote screen. These price changes seem to go invariably against the trader rather than in his favor. The fact that it can and does frequently occur in futures market, you should know that professional traders avoid market orders whenever possible.

Time Order

Orders are also limited as to the time they remain valid. You can enter a day order to be executed the first time the contract trades at your price. If this order is not filled by the close, the order is automatically canceled and a new order must be initiated the next morning if you still want the position.

Good Till Canceled (GTC) Order

Good till canceled is the type of order that is an open order. It will stay in the broker's deck (deck of orders) until it is filled or canceled.

All or None (AON)

The floor broker cannot fill only a portion of your order. He has to fill all contracts. It is a limit order that must be filled entirely. If, for example, you have a limit order to sell 10 March S&P 500 at 620.10 and you sell only 6 contracts because 620.10 was the high and your order could not be completely filled, you have to accept a partial fill. Some brokers may not accept an AON order.

Stop Orders

A stop order is particularly important in futures trading. It is used mostly to limit losses (Stop Loss) but it does have other applications. By determining at the outset, the amount of loss you are prepared to take and placing your stop order so your position is closed out at that point, you are using good trading discipline. Every time you place an order, you should also place a contingent open order to offset your new position. The second order would remain inactive until a transaction took place. If the market moves against you and "sets off your stop," then the open stop order becomes a market order. Just like and market order, there is no assurance that it will be executed at the stop price. If, for an extreme example, you were so unlucky and the market were to go "Up the limit" or "down the limit" through the stop level, you would be locked into your position until trading resumed at some price level. This scenario does not happen often but it is an inherent major risk of commodity futures trading

Where should you put a stop? The 33% retracement is common but usually too close. The 66% retracement is too much to give back to the market but a 50% retracement is a good place for a stop. The art of setting a stop price lies in deciding how much of an adverse price move is a temporary correction and when it becomes a reversal of a major trend.

Stop Limit Order

One variation of the Stop Loss order is the Stop Limit order. When the stop price is hit, the floor broker will hold a regular limit order instead of a market order. The order becomes a specific priced order. The disadvantage of a Stop Limit is that if the market falls or rises through the limit price, there is no assurance that the price will return to the level where it can be filled. If the market goes through your price and keeps on going, you will not get in

Market If Touched (MIT) Order:

This order becomes a market order if the market trades at or is bid or offered at the specific price. It is then filled just the same as a market order. A MIT to buy becomes a market order if and when a futures contract trades at or below the order price. A MIT to sell becomes a market order if or when a futures contract trades at or above the order price.

Spread Order

A spread is a simultaneous long and short position in the same or related commodity futures. A spread order would be to buy one month of certain commodity and sell another month of the same commodity, or buy one month of one commodity and sell the same month of another but related commodity.

Buy 5 May Corn/Sell 5 May Wheat
Buy 5 July Beans MKT/Sell 5 Nov. Beans MKT
Buy 5 July Beans/Sell 5 Nov. Beans 2 cents

The risk of trading spreads can be substantial. The high degree of leverage that is often obtainable in trading recognized spreads due to small margin requirements, can work against, as well as with you. But the spread trader has many advantages which include increased diversity of capital, flexibility, seasonal and historical reliability, frequently lower risk exposure and less violent price movement.

Market on Close (MOC)

Market on close is an order that is executed at the close of the market. The closing range is established during the last 30 seconds of the market day. There is a high and a low during that period and it is established by the "pit committee." A MOC order is a market order that is executed during the last 30 seconds of the trading day and must trade within the closing range. In conclusion, all orders, except market orders, can be canceled prior to execution. A market order is executed immediately upon entering the pit, so it is impossible to cancel. There are other variations of orders but the types addressed here are sufficient.

EXERCISE QUESTIONS

1. What are the differences between forward and futures contracts?

2. What is a performance bond?

3. What is an exchange?

4. Name the ways a trader can exit his futures position.

5. What is a hedger?

6. What is a speculator?

7. How do cash markets affect futures markets?

8. Name the government agency empowered to regulate the futures industry.

9. What is a market order?

10. What is a limit order?

11. What is a stop order?

12. What is a seat?

13. Futures have traded in the United States for hundreds of years. (True/False)

14. Forwards have traded in the United States for hundreds of years. (True/False)

15. A trader buys a Treasury Bond contract for 112-03 and sells it later for 112-13. How much has the trader earned?

16. What is the contract high and low for the December Japanese Yen contract?

2 THE 20 RULES OF COMMODITY FUTURES TRADING

Discipline, the key to success in so many aspects of life is the main ingredient of any successful trading plan. But what does discipline mean to an intra-day trader?

1. Discipline means taking small, quick losses and letting your profits ride.
2. Discipline means using stop loss orders on every trade to limit your losses and moving your stop loss orders to protect your profits.
3. Discipline means following all the buy and sell signals that your style of trade or system of trade offers.

In all trading you must expect losses and accept them gracefully. It may take only one mistake to wipe out the profits of ten winning trades. You cannot pick and choose which trading signals you are going to take and which you are not. Trading is not science - where exact things occur. If you are only 50% accurate with your trading, you can still bring home a boatload of money when you manage your losing positions correctly. This is true trading discipline. It is hard to want to continue trading after one, two or even three straight losses in a row. You take the signals and you lose money, but worst of all, you lose confidence.

If you pre-decide on every trade how much risk you are going to take (in other words, how much money you are willing to lose) you are using excellent trading discipline. If you seek a trading style that offers you not one-to-one risk to reward; not two-to-one risk to reward; but a three-to-one risk to reward ratio, you are using excellent trading discipline.

Commodity markets are a great place to make a small fortune; out of a large one. For every dollar made, a dollar is lost by some other trader. If you have the discipline to adopt a style of trade that offers a three-to-one risk to reward ratio, you will be able to be wrong on 75% of your trades and right on only 25% of your trades and still break even. This is a great approach, particularly for new traders.

One of the biggest problems that new traders must overcome is their expectation to earn money right away. They lose sight of the fact that commodity futures is a zero-sum game - that for every dollar made, a dollar is lost by some other trader. They forget that it took them a good deal of time to become proficient, let alone expert, at their previous career. They do not acknowledge that they are trading against experts with years of experience that come from multigenerational trading families. People whose parents, spouse, friends, siblings and children are also traders. People who eat, sleep, drink and virtually live for trading. It is hard to beat a professional in any field but in commodity futures you must learn before you earn.

The twenty Commodity Boot Camp, Ltd. trading rules that follow are meant to serve you. Discipline does not guarantee perfect results but it will keep you from second guessing your style of trading. Consistency and adherence to these rules is your best course of action.

THE TRADING RULES

Rule 1: Do not be a tradeaholic.

Rule 2: You trade to make money - not for fun and games or to escape boredom.

Rule 3: Never add to a bad trade.

Rule 4: Once you have a profit on a trade, never let it become a loss.

Rule 5: NO HOPING, NO WISHING, NO PRAYING. NO WOULD'VE, NO SHOULD'VE. NO OPINIONS!

Rule 6: Do not be a one-way trader - be flexible.

Rule 7: Know your risk on each trade. Trade with STOPS!

Rule 8: Look for a 3-1 profit objective before you make a trade.

Rule 9: When initiating a trade, always get your price.

Rule 10: When liquidating a bad trade always use a market order!

Rule 11: A scratch trade is a "winner."

Rule 12: Make ten points on a million trades - not a million points on ten trades!

Rule 13: Learn from your own mistakes.

Rule 14: Have a plan. Trade it. Monitor it.

Rule 15: The 3 losing trades in a row rule - Stop! Take a break.

Rule 16: DISCIPLINE! 90% of the public lose without it.

Rule 17: Pay attention to the weekly highs and lows!

Rule 18: Guru software systems only make money for the sales representatives. Develop your own approach.

Rule 19: Understand spreading and options.

Rule 20: Technical and fundamental indicators are equally important!

3 PIVOT TECHNIQUE

For an active intra-day trader, the Pivot Technique offers numerous trading opportunities. It works efficiently in all futures markets, but is especially effective in markets with a wide daily trading range. Markets with a regular wide daily trading range include the S&P 500, T-Bonds, Swiss Franc, Deutschmark Mark, Japanese Yen and British Pound, to name a few. The Pivot Technique is more difficult to use in the agricultural markets, which generally have narrow daily trading ranges.

The assumptions behind the Pivot Technique are simple and easy to follow, and the technique itself is useful because it forces discipline upon the trader. It also gives the trader an idea where prices may trend. The essence of day trading with the Pivot Technique lies in going long (or buying) when the market penetrates the pivot in a bull rally and going short (or selling) when the market penetrates the pivot in a down-side move. In this presentation, we will explain what these assumptions are and how you can calculate your own pivot points for trading. We will also explain how to implement the support and resistance numbers you calculate into your own trading strategy.

CALCULATING THE DAILY PIVOT

The entire Pivot Technique consists of five basic arithmetic and algebraic formulas. It is founded in the very basis of technical analysis; which is the previous market sessions' high, low and settlement (also known as closing) prices. In fact, the very first formula, which provides the daily pivot, requires you to gather the previous days' market high, low and closing prices, then add them together, and then divide the sum by three. These two relatively easy calculations will generate the daily pivot point and the pivot point will be used in all four of the other Pivot Technique formulas.

Futures prices fluctuate constantly during the day. We know by the end of the trading day there will be a high, a low and a closing price. However, we also would like to know what the average price was during the day. This average price can give us an idea whether we want to be long (buyers) or short (sellers) in the market. If a price were above the daily average, we would want to be long; conversely, if a price were below the daily average, we would want to be short. You should realize now that the daily average is synonymous with the daily pivot.

The Pivot Technique helps the trader by guiding him where to place his buy and sell trades. Using the Pivot Technique, we can pick prices where there is resistance and support. Resistance and Support refer to the tendency of price movement to revert back to the average. Resistance is defined here as sustained selling coming into a market to halt or subdue a bull rally. Conversely, Support is defined here as sustained buying coming into a market to halt a breakdown in price.

Prices generally do not trend beyond resistance and support points. If the price exceeds resistance or drops below support, we would interpret this as evidence of a trend. Resistance and support points do not predict price movement. They are used by the individual trader to initiate buy or sell orders.

Let us work with an example. Suppose the S&P 500 futures contract closed at 500, with a daily high of 502.50, and a daily low of 497.50. To determine the daily pivot, we calculate the average of the high, low and closing price. In this example, we add 502.50 plus 497.50 plus 500 and divide the sum by three. The average, or daily pivot is 500. During the trading day, we would tend to be long above 500 and short below 500.

RESISTANCE LEVEL ONE (R1)

To calculate the first resistance level (R1), we multiply the pivot by 2 and subtract the low. Using the same numbers as in our previous example, we multiply 500 by 2 and subtract 497.50. So 500 X 2 = 1000 - 497.50 = 502.50. Our answer is 502.50. So Resistance Level One (R1) equals 502.50.

SUPPORT LEVEL ONE (S1)

The first level of support (51) is calculated by multiplying the pivot by 2 and subtracting the high. We multiply 500 X 2 = 1000 and subtract 502.50 which equals 497.50. So 497.50 becomes our first level of support (51). We now have the beginning of a daily trading game plan. The numbers 502.50, 500, and 497.50 are Resistance Level One (R1), the Daily Pivot (P) and Support Level One (51), respectively.

As stated before, the essence of day trading the pivot lies in going long when the market violates the pivot in a bull rally and going short when the market violates the pivot in a bear break or downward move. If we got long when the market penetrated the pivot point in an up move, our first profit objective would be Resistance Level One (R1). We would use a trailing sell stop loss order to protect our long position that we initiated at the pivot point. If the market met resistance (that is selling pressure) at Resistance Level One (R1), we would sellout our long position for a profit and then cancel our protective sell stop loss order. But if the market penetrated Resistance Level One, we would stay with our long position and move our protective sell stop loss order to just below Resistance Level One (R1) and try to acquire more profit. Remember, and this is very important, resistance levels tend to become support levels once they are penetrated in an upward move!

Conversely, if we were to initiate a short position when the pivot point was violated in a downward move, we would trail a protective buy stop loss order to protect ourselves in a sudden market reversal, but our first profit objective would be Support Level One (S1). If the market continued downward and met support at Support Level One (51), we would buy in our short position for a profit and cancel our protective buy stop loss order. But if the market continued downward and penetrated Support Level One (S1), we would move our protective buy stop loss order to just above Support Level One (S1). Again, this is very important, support levels tend to become resistance levels once they have been penetrated in a downward move. If the market continues to move downward, we would continue to move our protective stop loss order down to acquire and protect more profits.

Support points are where a trader would expect buy orders to cluster during a downward trending market and resistance points are where a trader would expect sell orders to cluster during an upward trending market. Support and Resistance points can and do get penetrated but these are the first levels of support and resistance. This is how the formulas are used to calculate these points and how an astute trader would trade them. If prices were below the pivot point, our bias is to be short with a trailing protective buy stop loss order and if prices were above the pivot point, our bias is to be long with a trailing protective sell stop loss order.

There are two more important points for us to calculate. They are referred to as Resistance Level Two (R2) and Support Level Two (2).

RESISTANCE LEVEL TWO (R2)

Resistance Level Two (R2) is the last point you would expect to meet resistance in a rising market. We do not want to be short if the market penetrates Resistance Level Two (R2). To calculate Resistance Level 2, we take the pivot and subtract the Support Level One (51) number and add the Resistance Level One (R1) number. In our ongoing example, we would take 500 minus 497.50 plus 502.50, which equals 505. So 505 is Resistance Level Two (R2). If we stayed with our long position when the market penetrated Resistance Level One (R1), our next profit objective would be Resistance Level Two (R2). We would be using a protective sell stop loss order to protect our profits. But if the market met resistance at Resistance Level Two (R2), we would sell out our long position and cancel our stop loss order. If the market continued to trend upward and penetrated Resistance Level Two (R2), we would move our protective sell stop loss order to just below Resistance Level Two (R2) because resistance levels tend to become support levels once they have been penetrated in an upward trending market.

SUPPORT LEVEL TWO (S2)

The last number we need to calculate is Support Level Two (52). To calculate this number, we take the pivot and subtract Resistance Level One (R1) and add Support Level (51). In our ongoing example, we would take 500 minus 502.50 and then add 497.50. The answer is 495.00. So 495.00 becomes Support Level Two (52). If support (buying orders) is going to come into a downward trending market, it should be at Support Level Two (S2). You do not want to be long when Support Level Two is penetrated.

If we stayed with our short position when the market violated Support Level One, our next profit objective would be Support Level Two. If the market moved downward to Support Level Two and buying (support) came into the market, we would buy in our short position and cancel our protective buy stop loss order. If the market penetrated Support Level Two, we would move our protective buy stop loss order to just above Support Level Two (52) to protect the profits in our short position. Again, I must remind you that support levels tend to become resistance levels once they have been penetrated in a downward trending market. Any and all trading techniques are meant to be traded with stop loss orders. Very few of us have the means to be able to withstand the inevitable swings that occur in even normal market conditions. You must decide in advance how much you are
willing to risk on each of your trades. Remember, most traders lose because they lack discipline. Plan your trade and then trade your plan. Do not trade with your emotions or ego.

I recommend using a six-tick, $150, stop loss order when trading the S&P 500. In T-Bonds, I use a three-tick or 93.75 stop loss order, and in the major foreign currencies, I use an eight-tick or $100 stop loss order. These are not exact rules and they tend to change depending on market volatility. However, you must trade with a stop loss order.

When trading the Pivot Technique, you may enter the market at any of the five levels we have discussed. However, trading is not an exact science. It is art that uses science. Your opinion whether to be long or short will determine your profitability and your ability or willingness to take small losses will determine your overall success.

Remember, the market is never wrong. Only your opinions on the market can be wrong.

THE FORMULAS IN REVIEW

1. (High+ + Low* + Close*) -;-3 = Pivot
2. (2 X Pivot) - Low = Resistance Level One (R1)
3. (2 X Pivot) - High = Support Level One (51)
4. (Pivot - 51) + R1 = Resistance Level Two (R2)
5. Pivot - (R1 - 51) = Support Level Two

Now write all these numbers down:

1. _____ Pivot
2. _____ Resistance Level One (R1)
3. _____ Support Level One (51)
4. _____ Resistance Level Two (R2)
5. _____ Support Level Two (52)

Become familiar with economic news that will impact your trading position.

The risk of trading futures can be substantial. Margins are subject to change without notice. Minimum margins do not apply to spread positions. The highest degree of leverage that is often obtainable in futures trading due to small margin requirements can work against you as well as for you.

4 THE GREENSPAN STYLE
ANY MARKET, ANY TIME, MANY TIMES

What information do I need to trade the Greenspan Style?

- Today's opening range prices.
- Today's high and low prices.
- Yesterday's high. low and close prices.
- The weekly high and low prices.
- The recent major high and major low prices.
- The all time high and all time low prices.

THE GREENSPAN STYLE
Any Market, Any Time, Many Times
A Simple Approach to Day Trading

OPENING RANGE

The opening range is one of the daily constants in any market. It is established within the first 90 seconds and it cannot be changed all day. The market may move back and forth through the opening range many times during the day.

Each time the market violates the high or low of the opening range, it is showing direction. A trader would want to establish a long position if the market violates the high of the opening range and conversely, a trader would establish a short position if the market violates the low of the opening range.

A stop loss order would be put somewhere within the opening range, depending on how much risk the trader is willing to take. Halfway, or in the middle of the opening range, is a good place to stop yourself out, especially for beginners.

But if you sell the market when it violates the low, and then the market retraces and looks like it may go back through the high of the opening range, cover your position or reverse your position.

Remember, you can afford to be wrong about the market for small amounts of money many times. It is those times that you get stubborn and turn a small loss into a large loss that destroy you.

THE DAILY HIGH AND LOW

The daily high and low are established and change constantly throughout the day. You will watch the market make a new high or make a new low and then reverse itself and trade in the daily trading range.

The market also will make a new high-or a new low and then appear to run (trade fast) to a new level. These are called break outs.

There are many stop loss orders associated with the daily high and low. The amount of buy stop loss orders above the high of the day or below the low of the day will propel the market to a new level.

Many traders put in day sell orders and place a stop loss order right at or just above the high of the day. Sometimes their stop loss order is equal to their position (so they just take their loss) and sometimes they put in reversing stops to first take their loss and second to establish a new long position. The market is showing direction by making a new high or new low.

The same theory works for day buy orders. A trader will have a day buy order and have the stop loss order right at the low of the day or maybe the stop loss will be just below the low of the day. This all depends on how much risk you are willing to take. Again, many traders will simply take their loss by selling an equal amount of contracts that they are long and other traders will put in a reversing position stop loss order to establish a new short position. This kind of trader is looking for a break out. A break out occurs when the market goes through the high or low of the day and runs volatile or violently to a new and much higher or lower level. It is a very risky kind of trade, but it can be very rewarding.

Remember you must trade with stop loss orders because this style I teach does not work everyday. When you are right, you can be very right; but when you are wrong - small losses are your best friend. The risk of trading futures can be substantial and the high degree of leverage that is often obtainable in futures, due to relatively small margin requirements, can work against you as well as for you.

THE PREVIOUS DAY'S HIGH, LOW AND CLOSING PRICE

The previous day's high and low prices are excellent reference points to enter, as well as exit, the market. They are also constants in the market because you cannot change a previous day's high, low or closing price.

If you are short and the market is about to violate the previous day's high, you should cover your short to take your loss or reverse yourself and get long, because the market is showing direction.

If you are long and the market is about to violate the previous day's low, you should offset your long position and initiate a short position because the market is showing direction.

There are many stop loss orders associated with the previous day's high and low. Many traders key off these numbers because the previous day's high, low and close data are the basis of technical analysis and the foundation on which many pivot systems are built.

The previous day's closing price is very significant because the market is judged by how much higher or lower on the day it is using that figure. When the market goes from higher to lower on the day, it is violating yesterday's closing price on the down side. You would not want to be long.

When the market shows you a short term trend, go with it. The trend is your friend.

THE WEEKLY HIGH AND LOW

The weekly high and low are also of significant importance. They are also not constants in the market. There are many traders who key off the weekly high and low. Many traders, who trade with a little longer time frame, use these points to enter or exit the market. By going through the weekly high or low, the market is definitely showing direction. There will be many stop loss orders with traders both entering and exiting the market. By this, I mean a trader that is long may sellout his position when the market violates the low of the week or a trader may have a sell stop loss order below the weekly low (break out). A trader that is short will buy in his position at the weekly high or just above it, or have a reversing stop order to establish a long position (bullish). Some traders establish new positions with stop orders. When the market penetrates the weekly low or high, they enter the market with a stop order.

THE RECENT MAJOR HIGH OR RECENT MAJOR LOW

Every market has an all time high or an all time low. They are major numbers that all market players watch. If the market approaches an all time high or low, an astute trader would pay considerable attention to that market. A violation of a record price is a history making event and commands considerable attention. Also there must be a significant reasons to propel a market to its record price. You would not want to be short as the market goes on to make a record high. You do not know how high the new record high will be. The same is true for a record low. You would not want to be long when the market goes through its record low; the bottom could be a long way down.

If the market violates the low, take a short position and, conversely, if the market violates the high, take a long position. Always trade with stop loss orders in case the market does not follow through.

Unfortunately, the market does not trade near its record high or low very often so we substitute the market's most recent major high or most recent major low. All markets have them.

It could be the high that was made three weeks ago, or the low that was made during the federal budget negotiations.

There is some factor that made the major high or major low significant. These are key numbers to trade off of. You should try to get short as the major recent low is violated or get long when the major recent high is violated.

There will be many stop loss orders associated with these points in the market and also a lot of interest by professional traders looking to initiate new positions. Keep track of the major recent high and low. They are key areas to enter or exit the market. •

The risk of trading futures can be substantial. Margins are subject to change without notice. Minimum margins do not apply to spread positions. The highest degree of leverage that is often obtainable in futures trading due to small margin requirements can work against you as well as for you.•

5 INTRODUCTION TO OPTIONS ON FUTURES

There are 2 types of options. The first is the **call option**. A call option gives the buyer of the option the right, but not the obligation, to buy a specific stock,commodity, or index at a set price on or before a specific date. The seller of the option must deliver the stock, commodity, or cash to the buyer of the option if he decides to exercise his option. The second type of option is the **put option**. The buyer of the put has the right, but not the obligation, to sell a stock,commodity, or index on or before a specified date. The seller of the put option has the obligation to be long the stock,commodity,or index if the buyer of the put decides to exercise. The buyers of options exercise their rights while sellers are assigned.

The general characteristics of options are their **strike price, the expiration date, premium, time value, intrinsic value,** and **volatility.**

The **strike price** is the price the underlying stock,commodity, or cash index will be delivered if the option is exercised

The **expiration date** is the date after which an option cannot be exercised. Options can be either American style, where they can be exercised any day prior to expiration, or European style, where they can be exercised only on
expiration day.

The **premium** is the price paid for an option.

An option's market value is the sum of its intrinsic and time value. The intrinsic value is the value of the option if it were exercised immediately. The time value is the difference between the option's market price and its intrinsic value. Intrinsic values cannot be less than o. For call options, the option is in-the-money if the strike price is below the option's market price. A put option is in-the-money if the strike price is above the market price. For an out-of-the-money call, the strike is higher than the market price. For an out-of-the-money put, the strike is below the market price. At-the-money calls and puts have market prices approximately equal to their strike prices.

Volatility is a measure of future price uncertainty. There are 3 types of volatility. Historical volatility is a measure of price movements within a set period of time. Forecast volatility is an estimate of future price changes. Implied volatility is the volatility implied by using a theoretical pricing model. The major pricing models are the Black-Scholes model and the Binomial model. Black-Scholes is best used with European style stock options while the Binomial model is best used for American style options.

THE GREEKS

The Greeks refer to the letters of the Greek alphabet. The first letter, **delta,** is a measure of the rate of change in the price of an option with respect to change in the underlying asset. **Gamma** is the rate of change of the delta with respect to change in price in the underlying contract. **Theta** is the rate of change in the option's value for each passing day. **Vega** measures the sensitivity of an option to change in volatility. **Rho** is the rate of change with respect to changes in interest rates.

CHARACTERISTICS OF OPTIONS ON FUTURES

Options on futures, unlike options on stock, are options on an underlying futures contract. If a trader were to exercise his call option on his futures contract, he would be long 1 futures contract. If a trader were to exercise his call option on stock, he would be long stock. Options on futures are a derivative instrument based on another derivative instrument. Interest rates are not considered in options on futures because the futures contract tracks interest rates. The expiration month of the futures option contract does not necessarily correspond to the expiration date of the futures contract.

OPTION EXPIRATION GRAPHS

The following pages contain a major option strategy. The profit and loss is displayed for the position at expiration. **European style** options can only be exercised on expiration day, while **American style** options can be exercised anytime. Most options traded in the United States are American style. The vertical line represents potential profit and loss. The horizontal line represents the price of the underlying instrument.

It is our recommendation that before you put on a trade, that you know the potential profit and loss and the effect of time on the position.

While these graphs represent profit and loss on expiration day, the profit and loss for American style options changes constantly .•

EXERCISE QUESTIONS:

1. You buy a September call option that has a strike price of 100 on June 1 for $400. The underlying asset is trading at 95.
> a) Is the option in-the-money, at-the-money, or out-of-the-money?
> b) How much is the option's intrinsic value?
> c) How much is the time value?
> d) On the following day, your underlying asset is unchanged. Do you expect your option to be worth more or less?

2. On March 1, you purchased the June S&P 500 contract and want to insure your downside
> a) Do you buy a call or a put?
> b) If you write a call against your contract, are you covered or uncovered?
> c) If you buy a put and are long the contract, will you have to post more margin with your broker if the contract declines?

3. The delta of a long contract is always equal to _____

4. Time value is known as _____
> Time Value is an appreciating asset. (True/False)
> Gamma is how fast the option will change when the underlying asset changes. (True/False)

5. The delta of the following position is:
> Long 1 S&P 500 contract _____
> Long 2 S&P 500 contracts _____

6. Your friend tells you can buy his car for $5000 anytime within the next ten days. Do you have:
> a) a contract to purchase the car
> b) an option to purchase the car
> c) the right to sell the car
> d) the obligation to buy the car
> e) none of the above

7. On expiration day, you have an in-the-money D-Mark call option. A week later, you call your broker to check on the futures contract. He tells you:
> a) You don't have anything; why didn't you call?
> b) Your call automatically converted to the underlying contract.

8. A bullish call spread is:
> a) long a call, short a call at a higher strike.
> b) long a put, long a put at a higher strike.
> c) short a put, long a put at a higher strike.
> ci)

9. A bearish put spread is:
> a) long a call, long a put at same strike
> b) long a put, short a put at a lower strike
> c) short a put, long a call at a higher strike, short underlying asset

10. A short strangle is:
> a) long a call and put at the same strike and expiration date
> b) short a call and short a put at the same strike and expiration date
> c) long a call, short a put at the same strike and expiration date

LONG CALL AT EXPIRATION

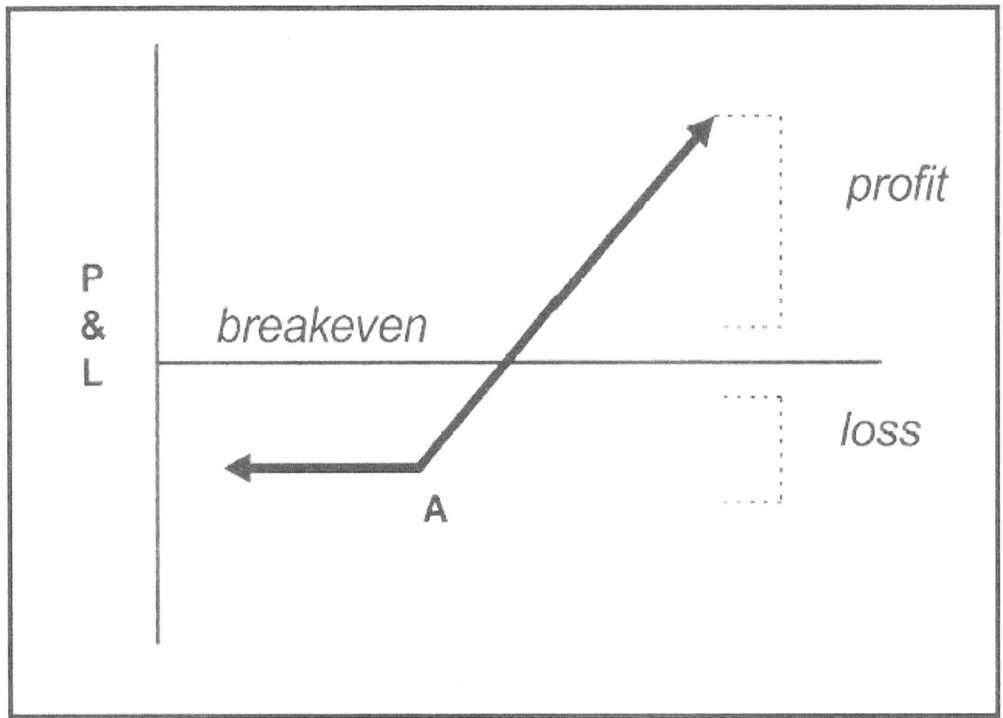

This position is used when a trader is very bullish. As the market rises, so does your profit. Your loss is limited to your option premium.

SHORT CALL AT EXPIRATION

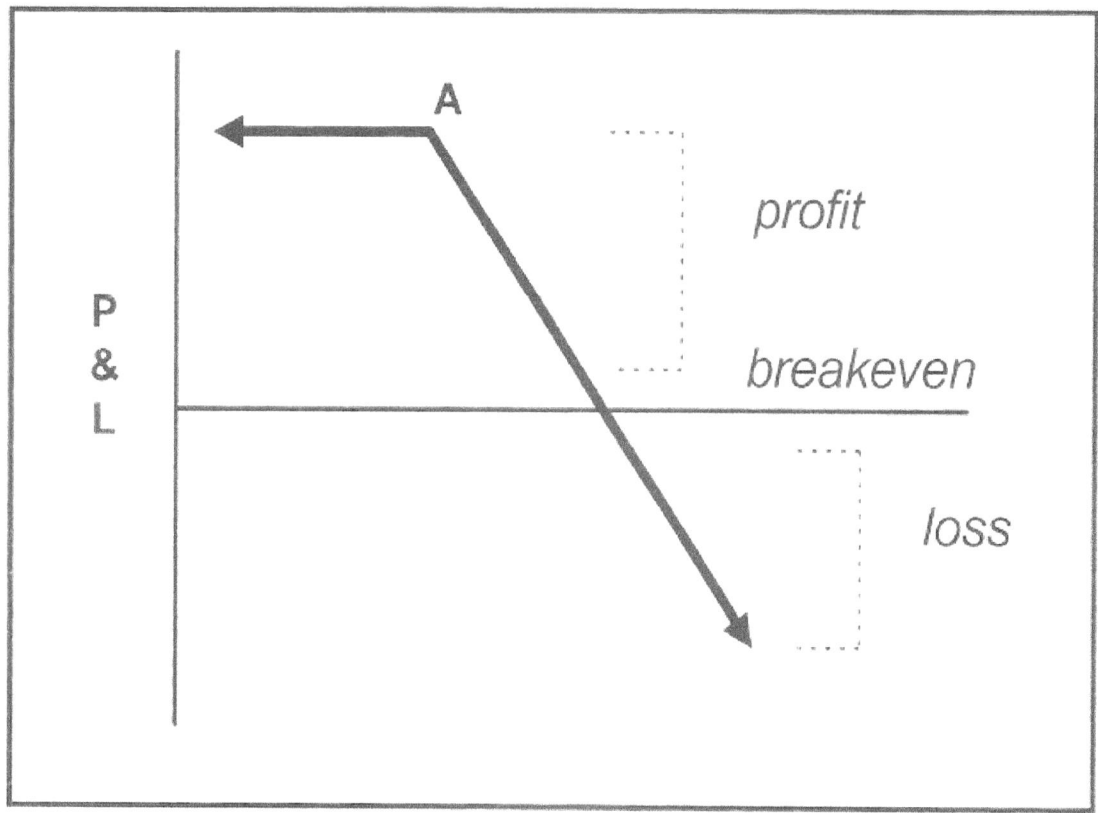

This is a neutral to bearish strategy. Profit is limited to the premium received. Breakeven is the strike price + premium received.

The risk is that if the market rises, the option writer faces potential unlimited risk.

Time is an asset. As time approaches expiration the potential profit approaches the premium paid.

LONG PUT AT EXPIRATION

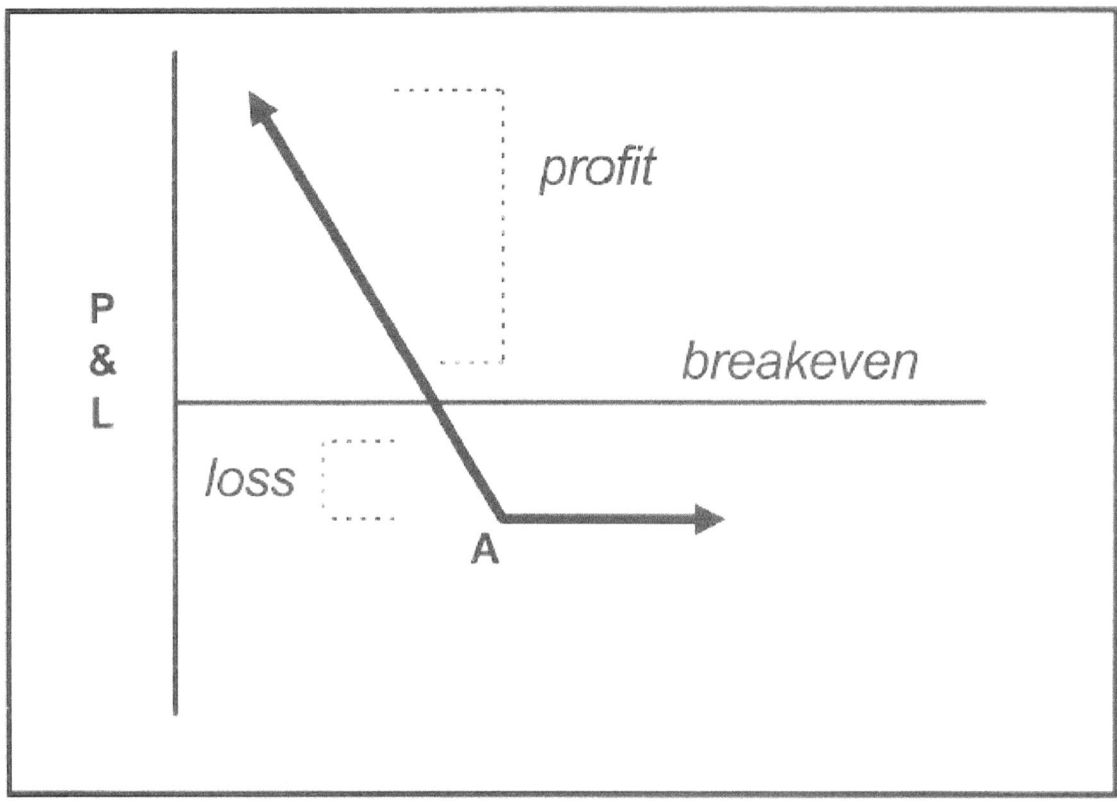

The opposite position of the long call. This is a bearish strategy. As the market falls, your potential profit increases. At expiration, the breakeven point is the exercise price - price paid for the option. The loss is limited to the amount paid for the option. Time is a wasting asset.

SHORT PUT AT EXPIRATION

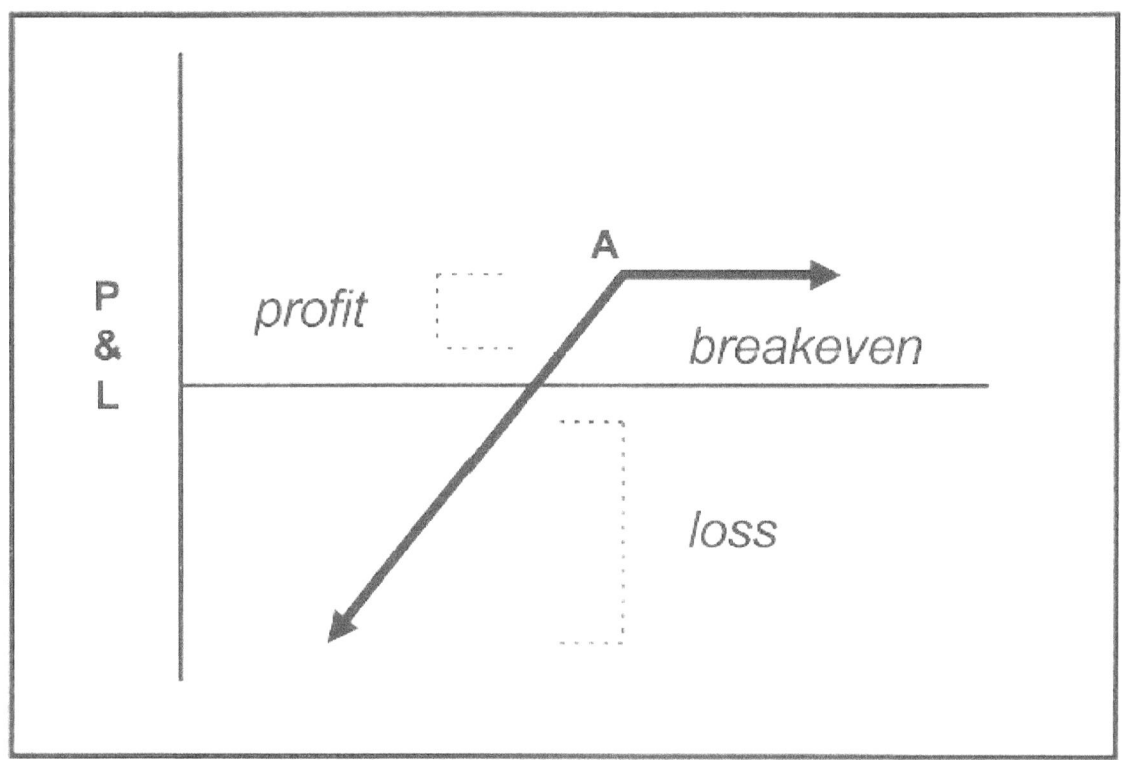

This is a neutral to bullish strategy. Profit is limited to the price received from the sale. Break even is exercise price - premium received. Time is a growing asset.

BULL SPREAD AT EXPIRATION

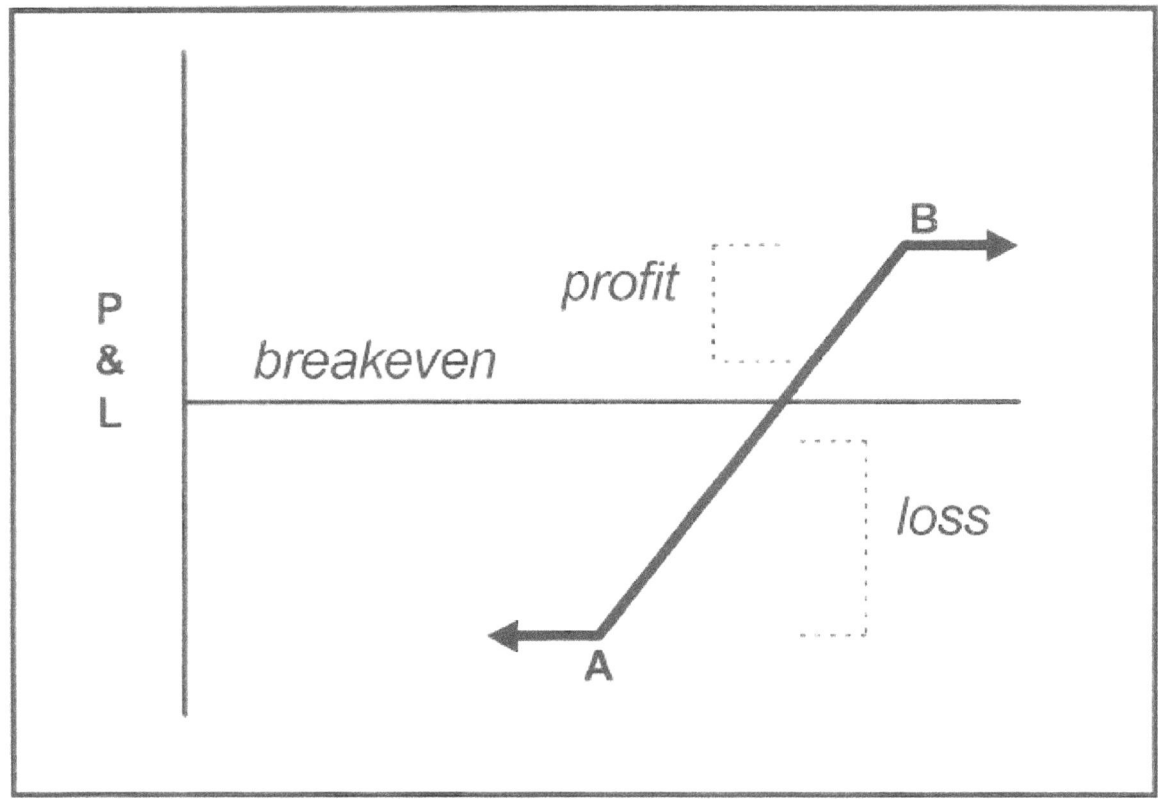

This is a bullish strategy with limited upside potential. Any strategy where one will profit if the market rises is a bullish strategy. The strategy can be implemented with calls, puts, and/or the underlying instrument. The most common implementation is being long a call at a lower strike and short a call at a higher strike price. In this case, the potential profit is the difference between the strikes plus the premium paid. The time effect depends on how far the market is to the strikes. At the strike where you are long time is an eroding asset. At the strike where you are short, time is a growing asset. The value of time fluctuates with the market.

Example Trades:
     Long a call at A, short a call at B
     Long a put at A, short a put at B

BEAR SPREAD AT EXPIRATION

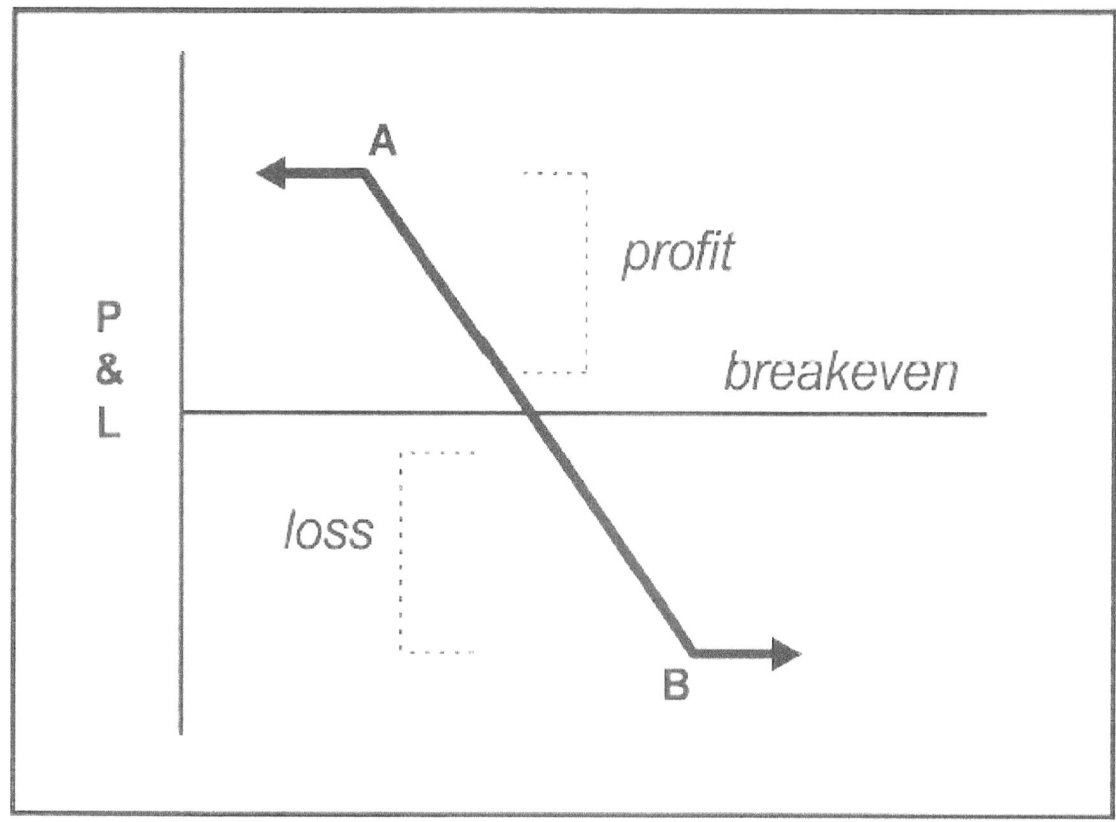

This is a strategy that is profitable if the market falls. It has limited profit potential. The most common way to implement the spread is to use puts being long at a higher strike and short at a lower strike. Like the bull spread, calls, puts, or the underlying asset may be used. Like the bull spread, the value of time fluctuates depending where the market is located relative to the strike prices.

Example Trades:
        Short a put at A, long a put at B
        Short a call at A, long a call at B

LONG BUTTERFLY AT EXPIRATION

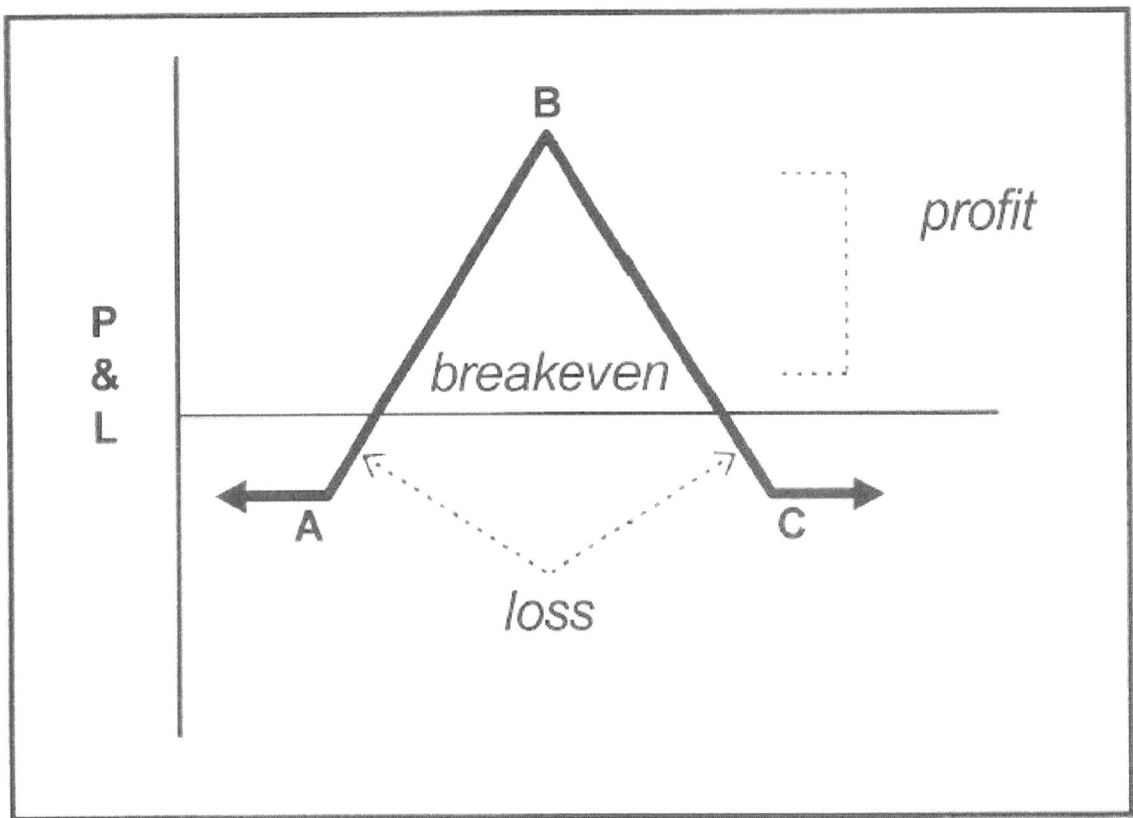

This strategy is a spread trade of 3 equally spaced options. All the options are either calls or puts. In this strategy, the trader is long at A and C and short at B. The ratio is always 1 by 2 by 1. At expiration the value is between 0 and the exercise prices. The loss is limited to the cost of the spread. Time decay is not a significant factor until the final month. This strategy is considered *very* conservative.

Example Trades:
       Long a call at A, short 2 calls at B, long a call at C
       Long a put at A, short 2 puts at B, long a put at C

(This distance between A and C must equal the distance between A and B.)

SHORT BUTTERFLY AT EXPIRATION

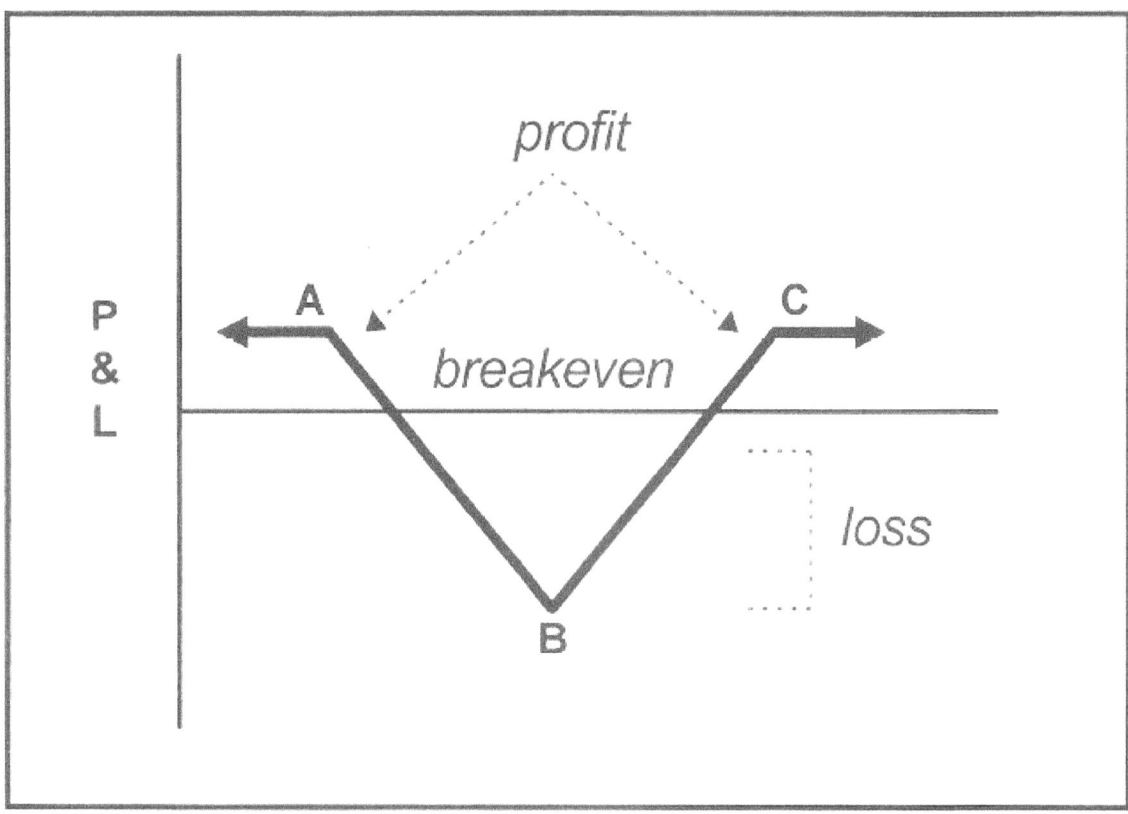

This trade is the opposite of the long butterfly. In this strategy, the trader is short at A and C and long at B. The profit and loss for the short butterfly is the same as the long butterfly.

Example Trades:
      Short a call at A, long 2 calls at B, short a call at C
      Short a put at A, long 2 puts at B, short a put at C

(This distance between A and C must equal the distance between A and B.)

LONG STRADDLE AT EXPIRATION

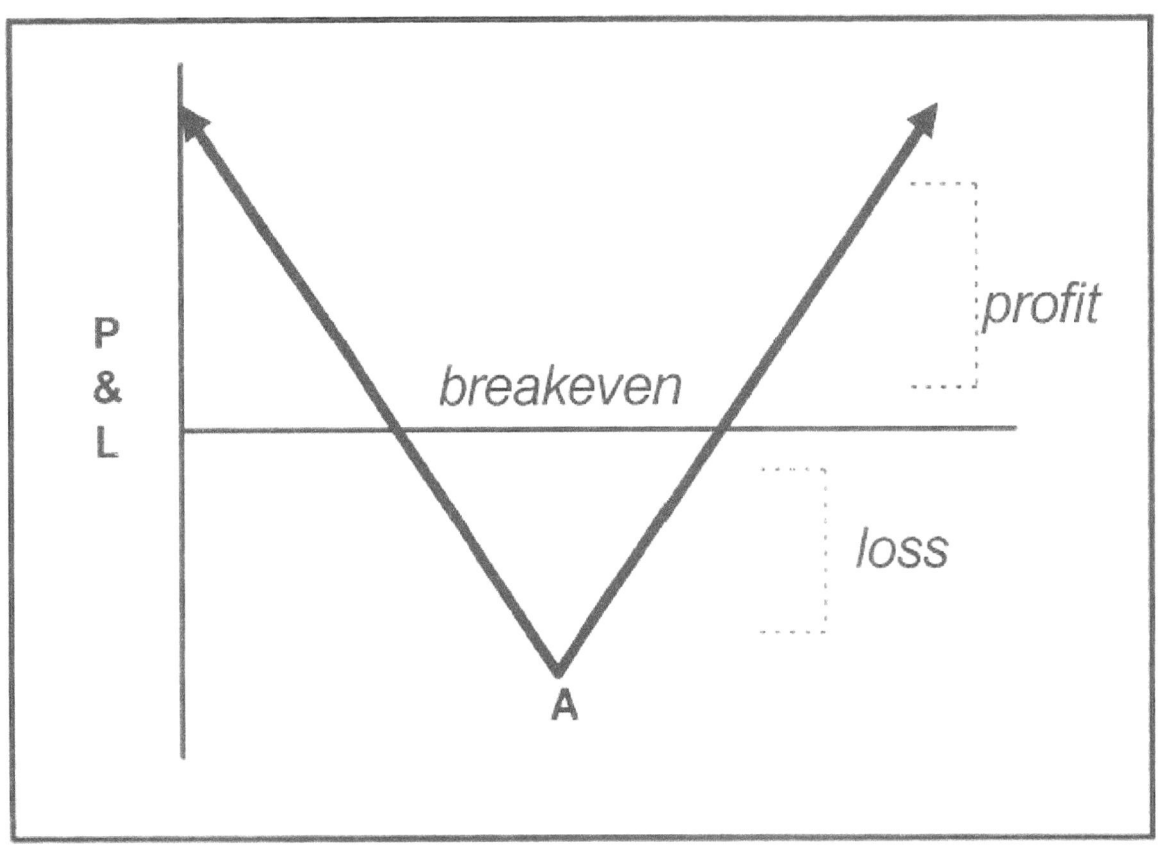

A long straddle is being long a call and long a put, all at the same exercise price and same expiration date. A trader is long a straddle if he is long puts and calls. Potential loss is unlimited, while risk is limited to the premium paid for the calls and puts.

This trade should be initiated delta neutral.

Example Trades:
　　　Long a call at A, long a put at A

SHORT STRADDLE AT EXPIRATION

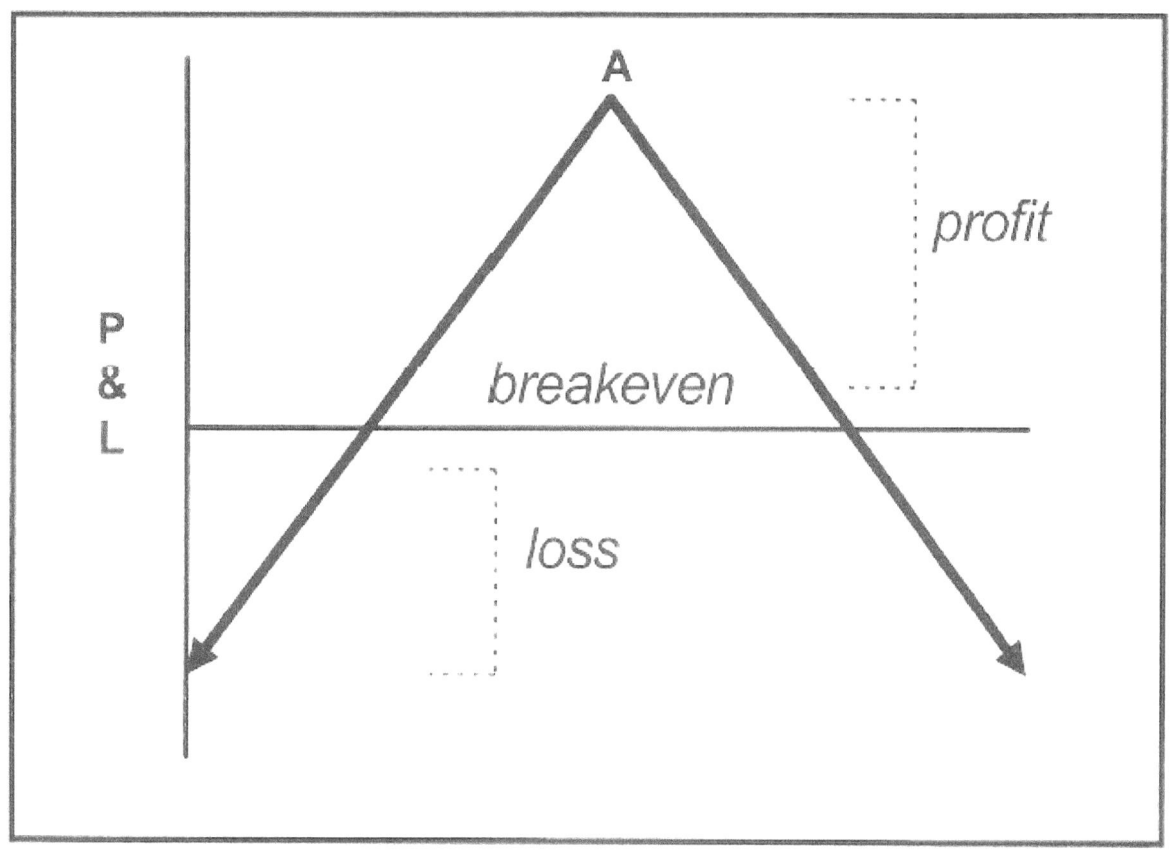

A short straddle is being short a call and short a put all at the same exercise price and same expiration date. A trader is short a straddle if he is short puts and calls. Profit is limited to the premium received for the puts and calls. Potential loss is unlimited. Time is an appreciating asset.

This trade should be initiated delta neutral.

Example Trades:
    Short a call at *A*, short a put at A

LONG STRANGLE AT EXPIRATION

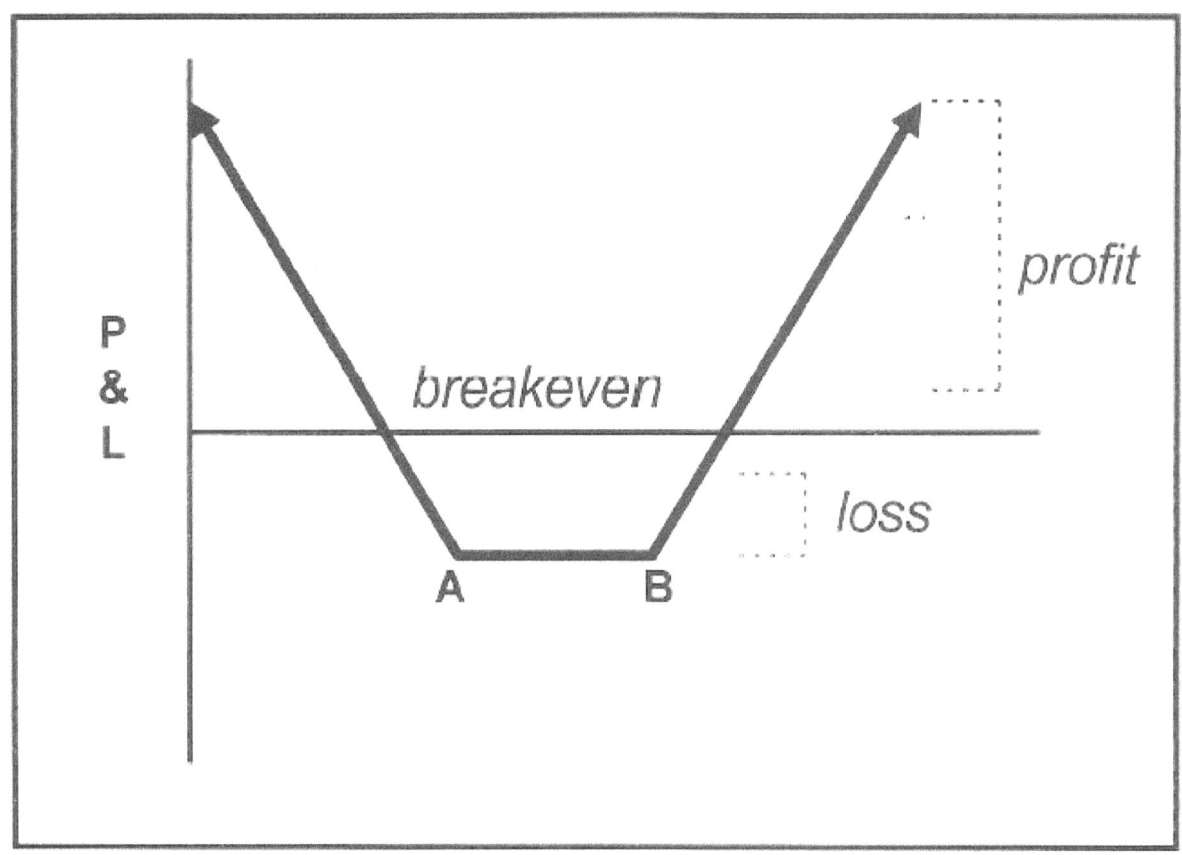

This strategy is used when the market has been relatively quiet for an extended period of time. A trader would use it to take advantage of any pending violent market moves.

Potential loss is limited to the amount paid for the put and call. He would not hold this type of position until it expires. Time is a wasting asset and erodes swiftly against the holder of this position.

One of the options must appreciate enough to recoup the amount paid to initiate the position.

This trade should be initiated at delta neutral.

Example Trades:
> Long a put at *A*, long a call at B
> Long a call at *A*, long a put at B

SHORT STRANGLE AT EXPIRATION

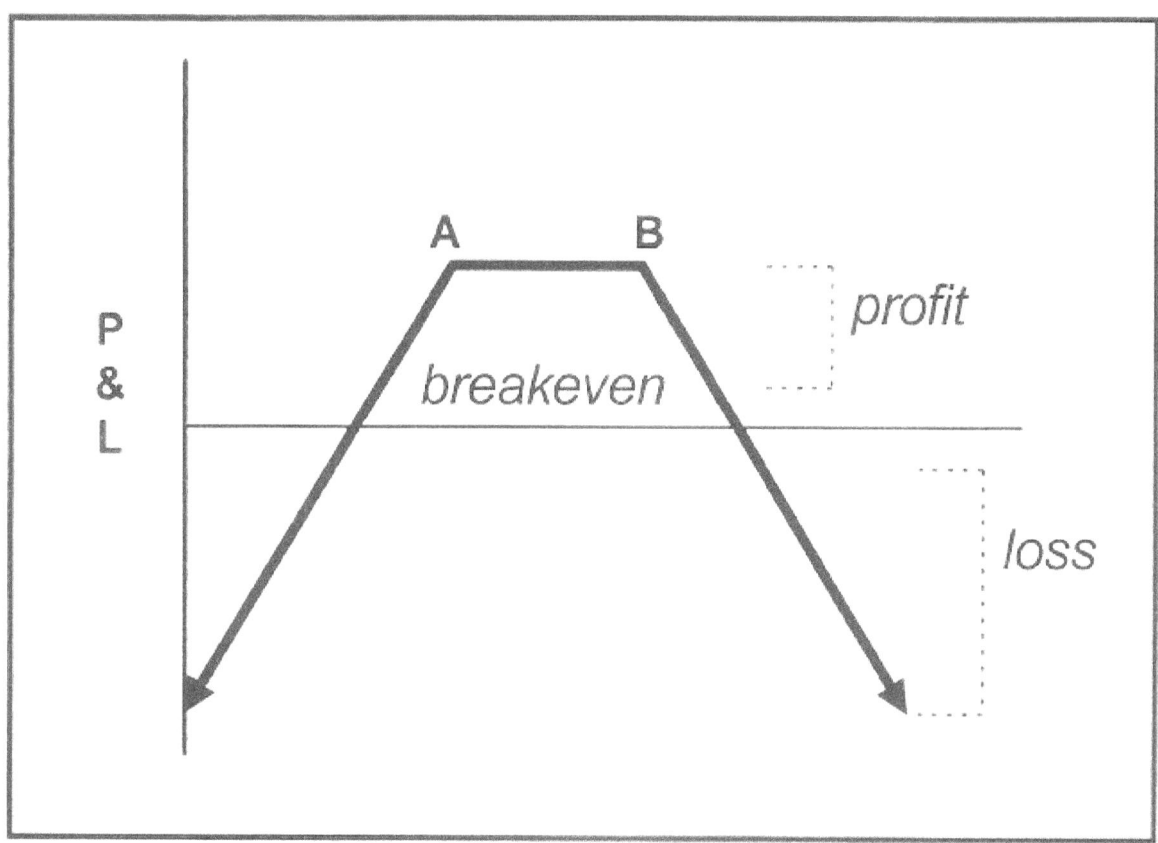

This strategy is used when the market has been relatively quiet for an extended period of time. A trader would use it on the assumption that the market will remain as quiet or quieter.

Potential loss is unlimited while potential profit is limited to the premium received at the initiation of the position.

He would not hold this type of position until it expires. Time is an appreciating asset.

While this strategy will prove profitable a majority of the time, if not managed properly can ruin a trader during periods of unexpected volatility.

This trade should be initiated at delta neutral.

Example Trades:
    Short a put at A, short a call at B
    Short a call at A, short a put at B

RATIO CALL SPREAD AT EXPIRATION

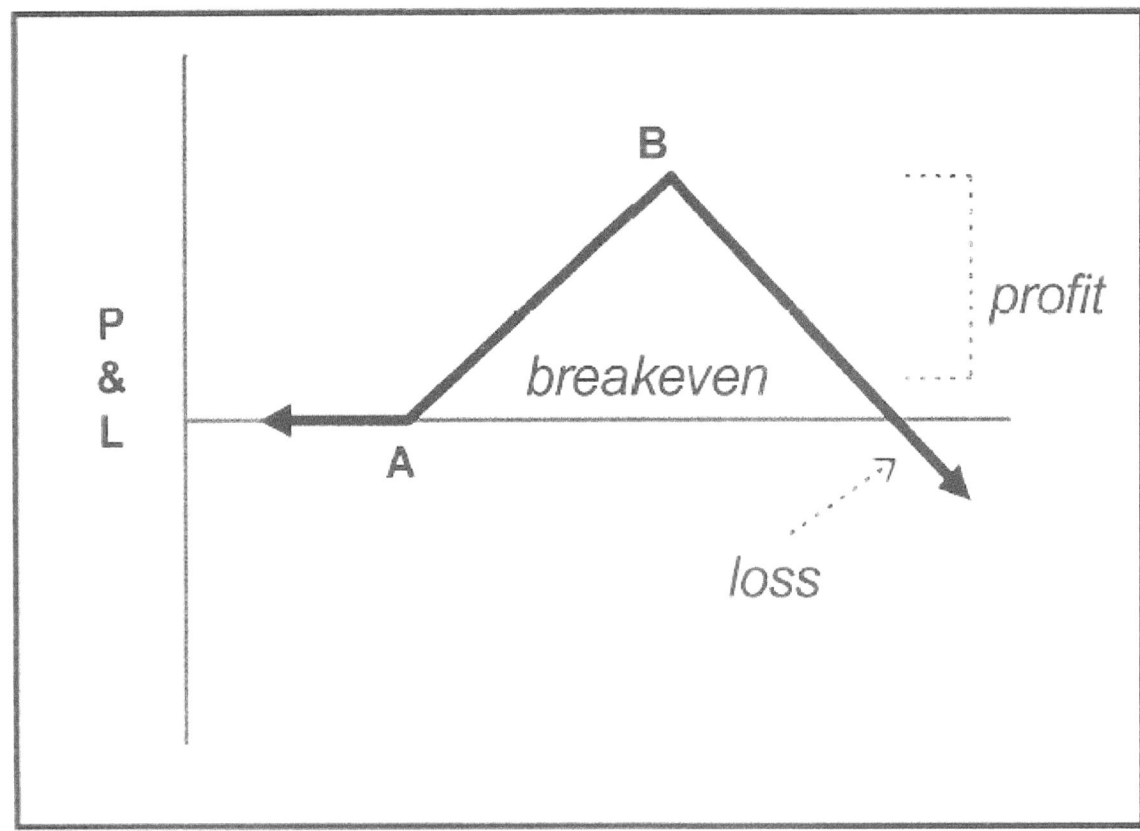

This spread is used when the market is at A and the trader expects a sell off. The risk on this trade is that the market may rally and expose the trader to the risk of any naked short position.

Time decay is a appreciating asset because the trader has more short positions than he has long.

This trade should be initiated at delta neutral.

Example Trades:
        Long a call at *A,* short calls at B

RATIO PUT SPREAD AT EXPIRATION

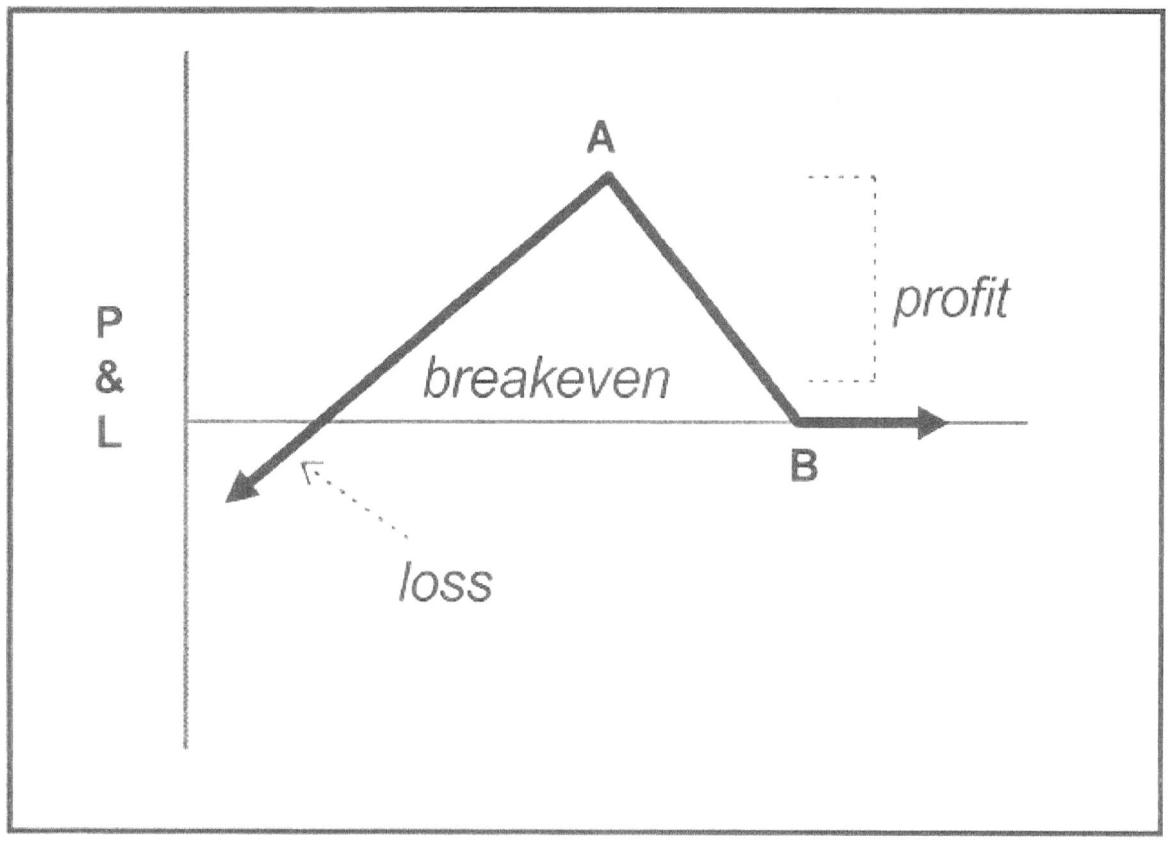

This spread is used when the market is at B and the trader expects a market rise. The risk on this trade is that the market may fall and expose the trader to the risk of any naked short position.

Time decay is an appreciating asset because the trader has more short positions than he has long.

This trade should be initiated at delta neutral.

Example Trades:
    Long a put at B, short puts at A

CALL RATIO BACKSPREAD AT EXPIRATION

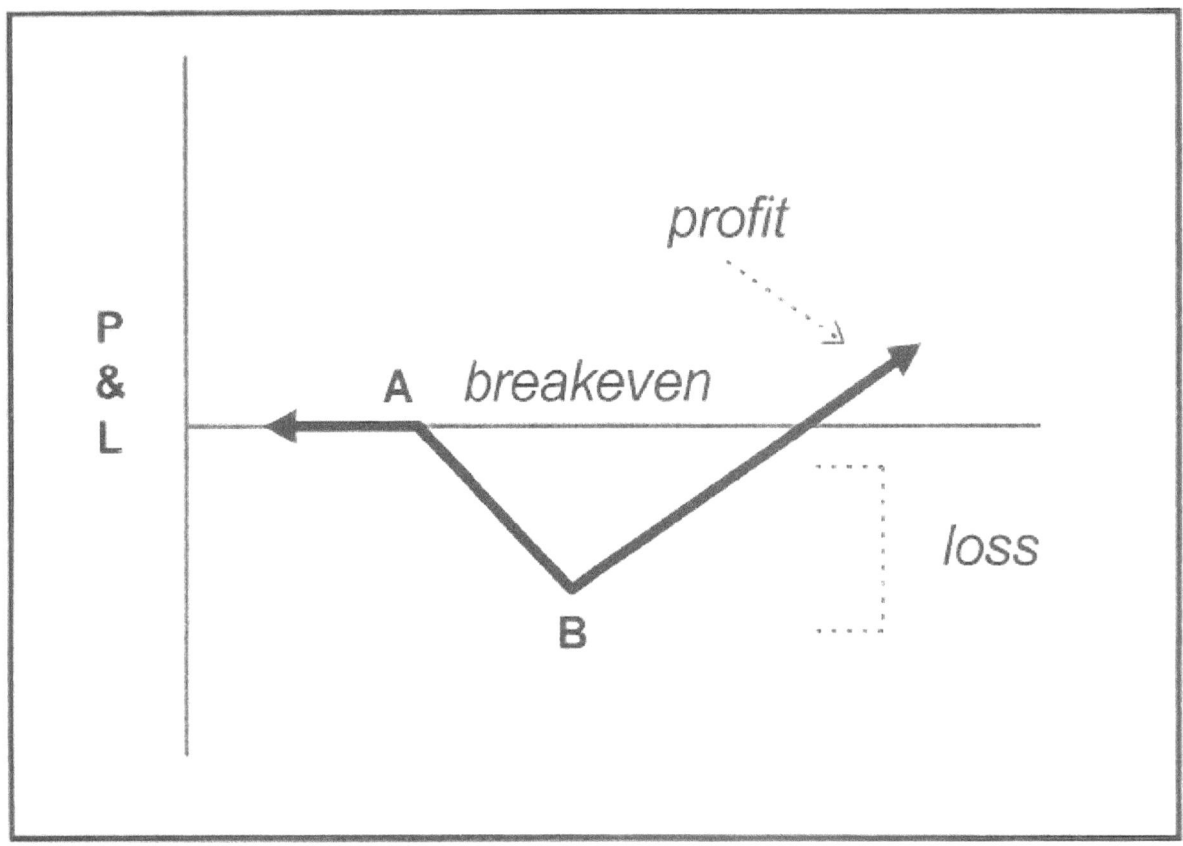

This trade is used when the market is near B and the trader believes the market will move upward.

The profit potential is unlimited and the risk is limited to the difference between B and A and the initial credit.

This position is considered to be less risky because the trader is net long on the entire position.

This trade should be initiated at delta neutral.

Example Trade:
    Short a call at A, long calls at B

PUT RATIO BACKSPREAD AT EXPIRATION

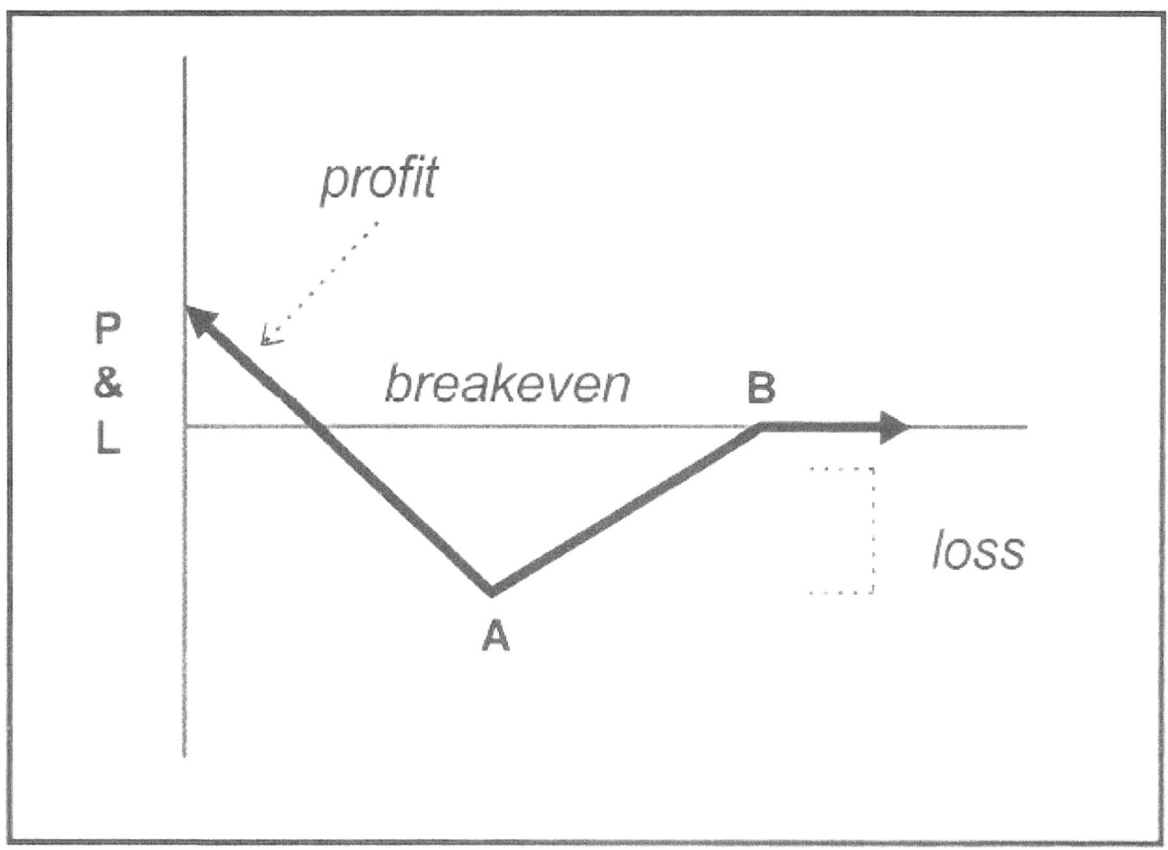

This trade is used when the market is near A and the trader believes the market will move downward.

The profit potential is unlimited on the downside and the risk is limited to the difference between B and A and the initial credit.

This position is considered to be less risky because the trader is net long on the entire position.

This trade should be initiated at delta neutral.

Example Trade:
    Short put at B, long puts at A

6 INTRODUCTION TO TECHNICAL ANALYSIS

Technical analysis studies price movements rather than the effect of supply and demand. To a technical analyst, all he needs to know about a market is contained in its price movements. It does not matter how or why prices are at their current levels, it only matters that they reached those levels. A technical analyst feels he cannot analyze the millions of factors that affect markets. Technical analysis focuses its attention on 3 factors: Price, volume, and open interest.

Price information is the most important component of technical analysis. Our discussion of price will cover moving averages, oscillators, stochastics, and Fibonacci numbers.

MOVING AVERAGES

Moving averages are used to detect changes in trends. The moving average is an average of a set of consecutive prices that is recomputed as new prices become available. For example, to compute a 5 day moving average, we would need prices from the last 5 days. Tomorrow, we would take the average of the prior 5 days. Let's consider a simple example. Suppose the prices for the last 5 days were 1,2,3,4,5. The 5 day moving average would be 3. 1 +2+3+4+5 divided by 5. Suppose the closing price tomorrow is 6. Our 5 day moving average is computed by taking 2 + 3 + 4 + 5 + 6 divided by 5. Our 5 day moving average is 4. Moving averages increase as the trend increases and they decrease as the trend decreases. Moving averages can be used to signal buy or sell decisions. For example, a trader may want to buy if his 5 day moving average crosses his 10 day moving average. Conversely, a trader may want to sell if his 10 day moving average crosses his 5 day moving average.

OSCILLATORS

Oscillators are used in non-trending markets. They are used to indicate overbought and oversold conditions. Oscillators try to measure market momentum. The faster prices change, the higher the momentum. However, we can't always tell what is a high value oscillator and what is a low value oscillator. The relative strength index, or RSI, provides guidelines for when markets are overbought or oversold. Values above 70 are considered potential tops and values below 30 are potential bottoms.

STOCHASTICS

Stochastics are a type of oscillator. The observation behind Stochastics is that as prices increase, closing prices tend to be at the top of price band and as prices decrease, they tend to be at the lower end of the price band. There are 2 important lines in Stochastics: %K and %0. %K gives you an idea if prices are at either the top or bottom of the range. %0 is a 3 day smoothed version of %K. %0 and %K vary between 0 and 100. According to theory, the best time to buy is when the %0 value is in the 10-15 area and the best time to sell is in the 85-90 area.

FIBONACCI NUMBERS

Fibonacci numbers are elements of the number series 1,1,2,3,5,8,13, ... Starting with the number 2, any number is the sum of the prior 2 numbers. The ratio of any number to the number preceding it is 1.618. The ratio of any number to the subsequent number is 0.618. Fibonacci numbers appear throughout nature. It appears to be a constant, much like pi or natural logarithms.

Ralph Elliott applied Fibonacci numbers to the stock market. He felt stock prices move in definite Fibonacci patterns. Researchers after Elliott have applied his analysis to the futures markets.

VOLUME

Volume can be an indicator of a market's direction and strength. Volume is the number of contracts traded in a specific period of time. The market is said to be bullish if volume increases with rising prices. If prices are falling and volume increasing, the market is said to be bearish. Our recommendation is to keep it simple. Prices rise when buyers are more aggressive than sellers and fall when sellers are more aggressive than buyers.

OPEN INTEREST

Open interest is the total number of outstanding contracts at the end of the trading day. It takes a buyer and a seller to change open interest. Money is flowing into the market when open interest increases. Traders are entering the market and holding their positions.

If prices are rising and both volume and open interest are increasing the market is said to be strong. In all other situations, the market is said to be weak (falling prices and/or falling open interest and volume).

CONTRARY OPINION

The theory of contrary opinion says essentially not to follow the crowd. Whenever a market maven touts a potential market move, consider taking the opposite position.

Many services report the number of investment advisors who are either bullish or bearish. A majority of advisors who are bullish can be interpreted as being overbought. A trader would then look to sell. An example would be the S&P 500 contract. When the DOW broke 5000, market touts said the market would stand still. Instead, over the next week, the DOW rallied 177 points. The problem with opinions is that everyone has one. Only the market will prove to be ultimately correct.

BAR CHARTS

The most common method of charting commodity prices is on a bar chart. Look at example 1. As you can see time is on the horizontal axis and price is on the vertical axis. Each vertical line represents 1 time period. This time period can be daily, weekly, monthly, or intraday. The hash mark on the left side of the bar represents the opening price for the specified time period. The hash mark on the right side of the vertical bar represents the closing price for the specified time period. The distance between the top of the bar and the bottom represent the period's price range from high to low. The price scale of the chart will be determined by the range and volatility of the particular market. Once these charts are constructed, we can study its patterns to help us trade. We can also use some elementary statistics to understand the charts.

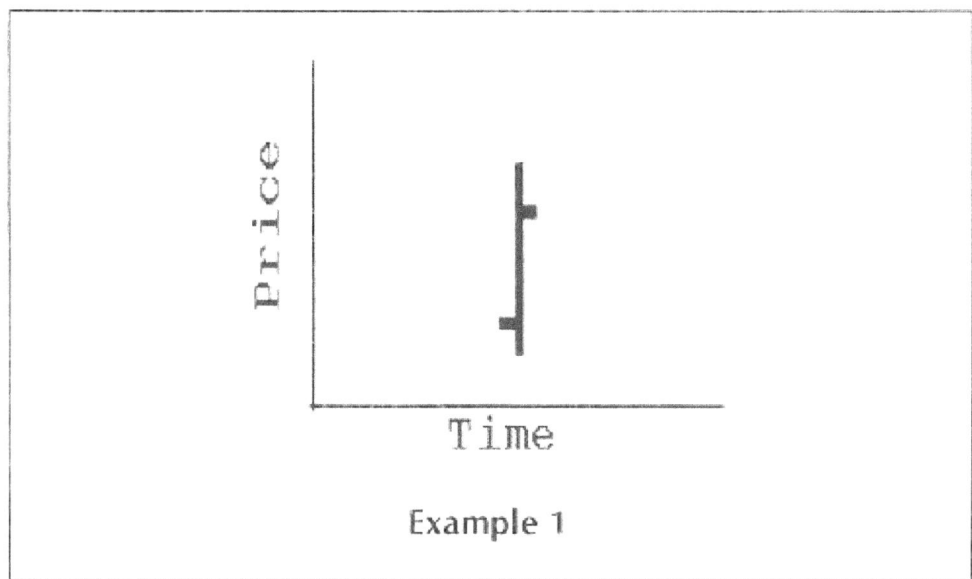

Example 1

Some of the chart patterns we will use to help us trade are Support and Resistance, Trend lines and Channels, Patterns, and Gaps. After the prior day's high, low, and close, support and resistance are the most significant signals for a technical analyst. Support and resistance points can be found at prior day's highs or lows, weekly highs or lows, or contract highs and lows. Support can also be found at other calculated areas, but they are not as important as the points we just mentioned. Support is simply the area where buy orders exceed sell orders so that a falling market ceases to fall. Resistance is where sell orders exceed buy orders so that a rising market stops rising. Once a support point is violated, it tends to become a resistance point. Once resistance points are violated, they tend to become support. **Highs, lows, and closes form the basis of all technical analysis and are one of the foundations of the Commodity Boot Camp, Ltd. style of trading.**

TRENDLINES

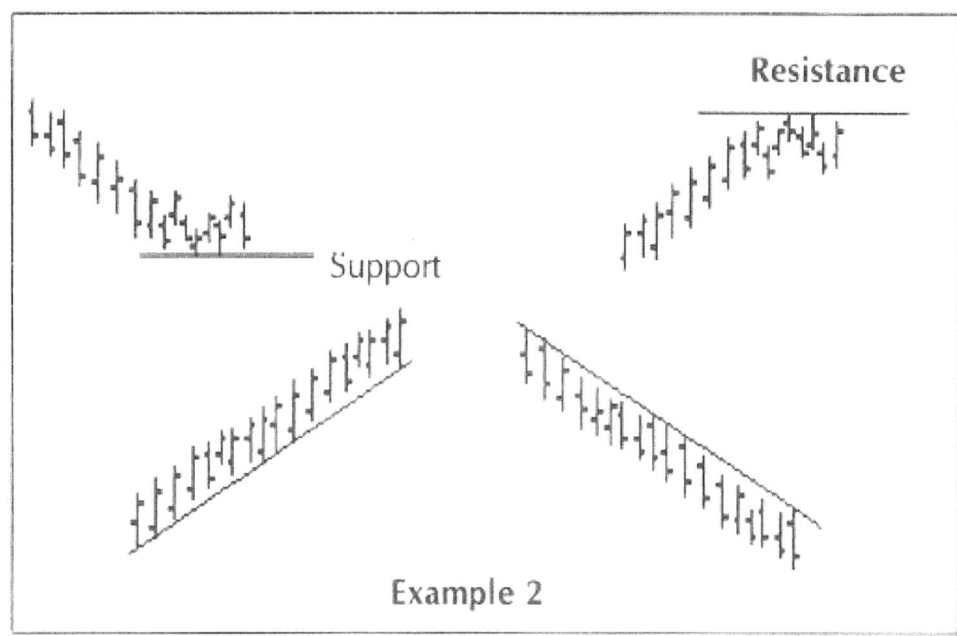

Resistance

Support

Example 2

A market that is making higher highs and higher lows is in an uptrend. Conversely, a market that is making lower highs and lower lows is in a downtrend. A trader would want to have more long positions in a market that is in an uptrend, while he would want to have more short positions in a market that is in a downtrend. While not precise, it is a good rule of thumb to examine your trades periodically and make sure you are not fighting a trend. Remember, the trend is your friend.

CHANNELS

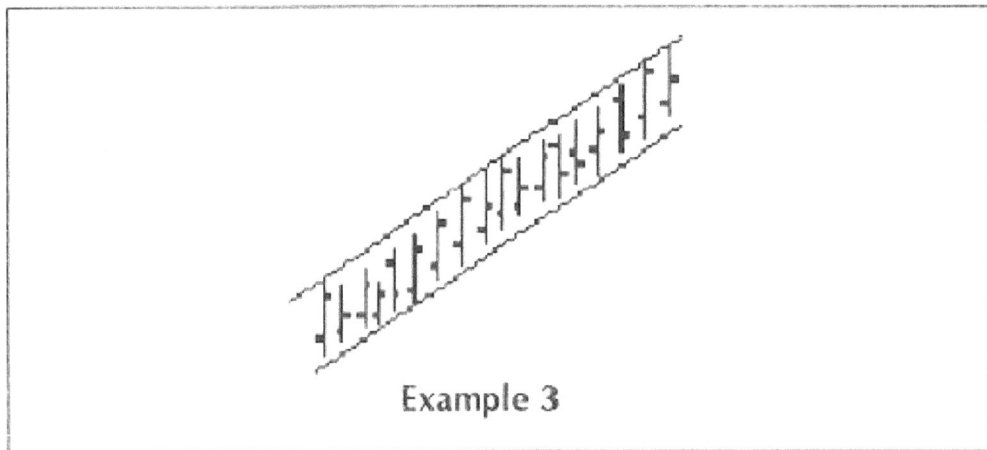

Example 3

Channels are trends that contain the price movement of an uptrend or downtrend. Channels are constructed by drawing a parallel line to the trend line from an intervening high along an uptrend or lows along a downtrend. The market price will tend to stay between these two lines as long as the market retains the current trend.

BAR FORMATIONS

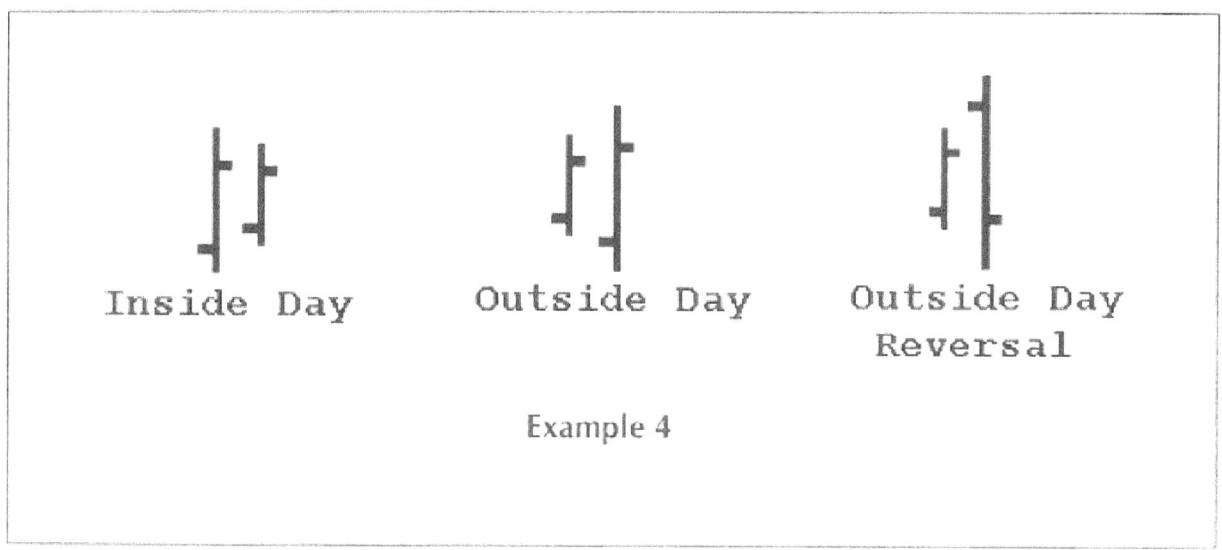

Inside Day   Outside Day   Outside Day Reversal

Example 4

There are 3 basic bar formations. The first is the inside day. The inside day is when the high and low of the trading day is less than the high and low of the prior day. For example, suppose the high and low of your market were 10 and 5. The next trading day, the high and low was 9 and 6. The trading day with a high of 9 and a low of 6 is said to be an inside day. You generally want to be active when the market violates any prior day lows or highs. The next bar formation is the outside day. The outside day is when the next trading day's high is greater than the prior day's high and the day's low is lower than the prior day's low. Once again, you would tend to be a buyer if the market settles near the high and you would tend to sell if the market settles near its low. The last formation is the outside day reversal. On this type of day, the close is below the prior day's low or the close is above the prior day's high.

CONTINUATION PATTERNS

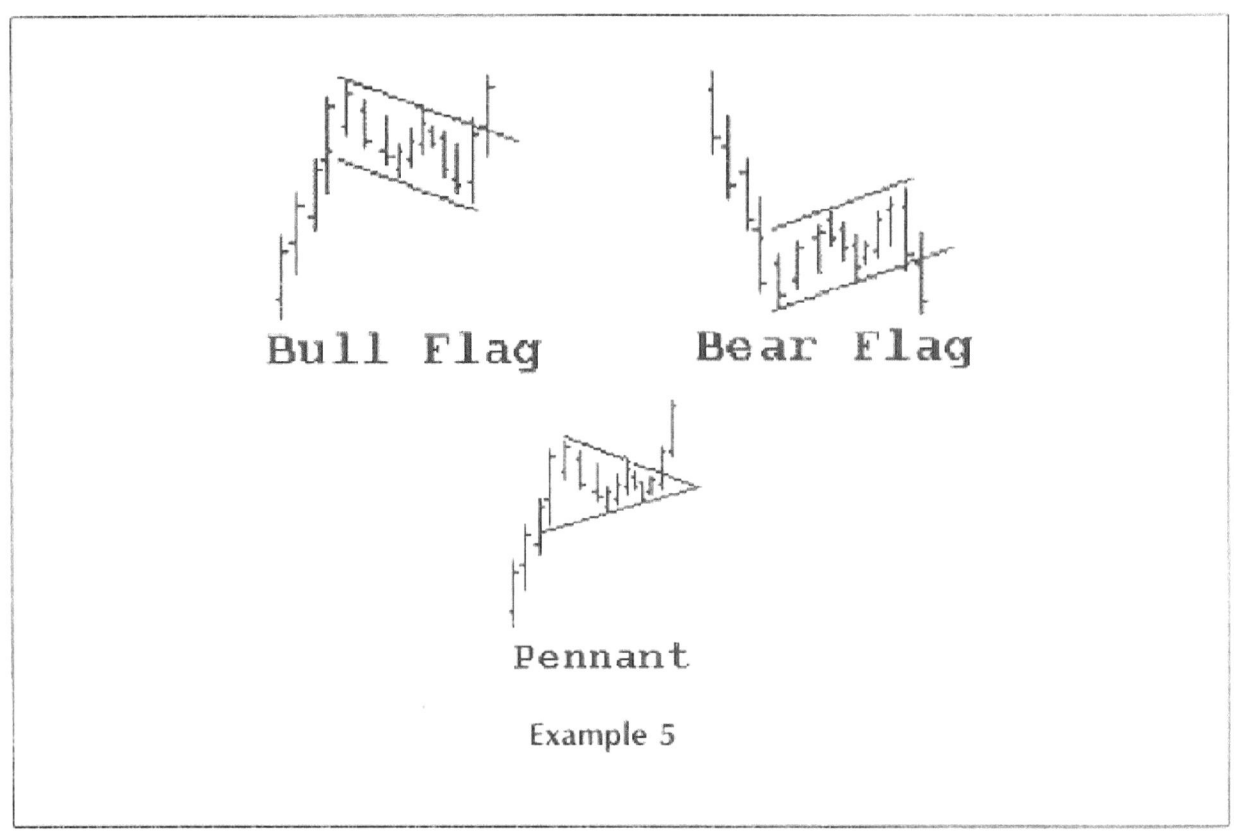

Bull Flag   Bear Flag

Pennant

Example 5

Continuation Patterns are patterns that are short term in duration and are a pause in a trend. An example of the continuation pattern is the S&P 500 market in 1995. Overall, the market was in an uptrend. However, there would be days where the closing price would not change by more than 5%. Those days would be seen as a continuation pattern on a chart. The most common type of continuation pattern are flags and pennants. Flags look like rectangles that have the same slope as the trend. Pennants look like triangles lying on its side. Flags and Pennants are usually found during times where the volume is falling in a market while traders are pausing to reconsider the trend in the market Usually, flags and pennants last no more than 2 weeks.

GAPS

Gaps are more correctly called price gaps. They are areas where no trading has taken place. There are 4 types of gaps: common, breakaway, runaway, and exhaustion.

Common gaps occur in thinly traded markets. They are not considered significant.

Breakaway gaps usually signal a pending market move. Breakaway gaps often signal a reversal of a trend and occur on heavy volume. Upside gaps will act as support areas on market corrections while downside gaps act as resistance areas. Runaway gaps give signals of a markets strength or weakness. In an uptrend, they are a sign of strength while in downtrends, they are a sign of weakness. They are also called measuring gaps because they signal the midpoint of a move.

Exhaustion gaps occur near the end of a trend. Once you have identified the breakaway and runaway gaps, an exhaustion gap is nearby. In an uptrend, prices will move quickly, as if they are in their last gasps, and turn lower just as fast. Exhaustion gaps are often discovered after they have made their move. You should use other technical indicators to confirm if a trend is terminating.

HEAD AND SHOULDERS

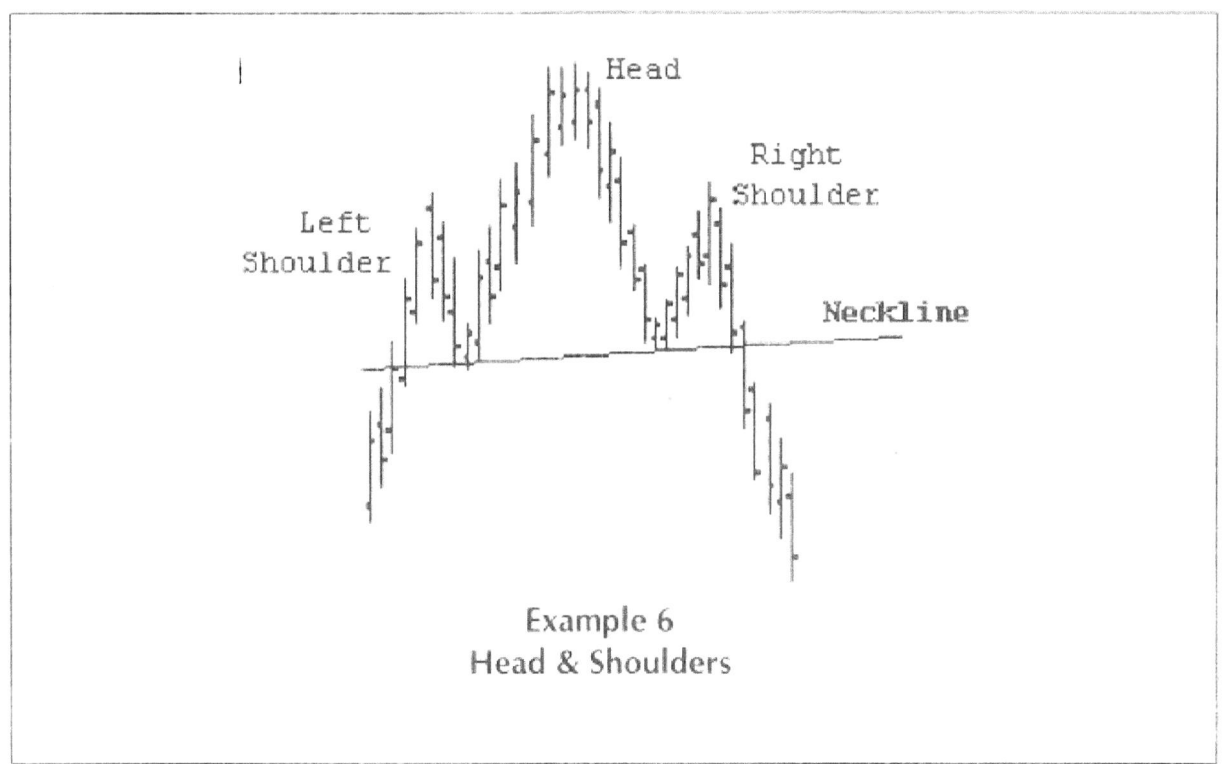

Example 6
Head & Shoulders

The head and shoulders top is a reversal pattern. **It** consists of a rally at a new high which fails, a rally to higher highs and a pullback. Ideally the left and right shoulder will be about the same height. A neckline is then drawn from the prior lows of the shoulders. This pattern is confirmed if the neckline is broken. The price objective for this pattern would be measured from the top of the head to the neckline and then this same distance would be projected from the break of the neckline.

DOUBLE TOPS AND BOTTOMS

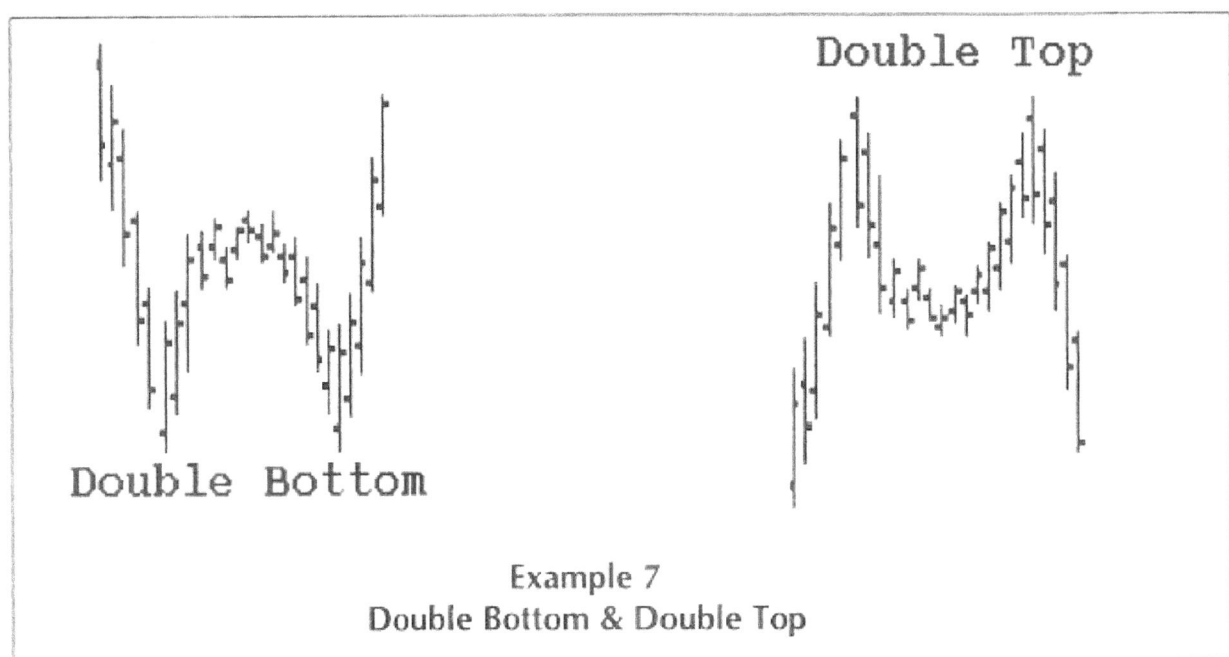

Example 7
Double Bottom & Double Top

A double top occurs when a rally stops at approximately the same level as previous rally and then fails. This pattern is not actually complete until the intervening low between the 2 highs is violated. Price objectives for this pattern are determined by measuring the distance from the highs to the intervening low and projecting 100% in price from where the market takes out the intervening low. The double bottom is taken by measuring the distance from the highs to the intervening low and then projecting 100% in price from where the market takes an intervening high.

CONCLUSION

Technical analysis is a wide area of research. It is our suggestion that you pursue technical analysis and use some of the tools when you analyze the markets. You should know how volume and open interest can affect prices and if trends are valid.

Moving averages are used to detect changes in trends. The moving average is an average of a set of consecutive prices that is constantly recomputed as new prices become available. Moving averages are reported on most major quote services. Moving averages are not useful in choppy markets.

In choppy markets, oscillators are useful. Oscillators measure market momentum. Oscillators increase or decrease in markets that are changing rapidly.

Stochastics are a type of oscillator. The idea behind Stochastics is that as prices increase, closing prices tend to be at the top of price bands and as they decrease, they tend to be at the lower end of the price band.

Contrary opinion states that a trader should not follow the crowd's opinion. If everyone agrees that the market is going in one direction, a trader should consider taking the opposite position. While contrary opinion is a subjective measure, it is useful to know where the crowd thinks the market is going.

Fibonacci numbers were developed by a 12th century mathematician. The summation series 1,1,2,3,5,8,13,21 is called a Fibonacci series. Fibonacci series are found in the rings of redwood trees and petal formations in certain plants. Ralph Elliott applied Fibonacci numbers to the stock market. Later, researchers extended Elliott's research to the futures market. Elliott's interpretation of Fibonacci's numbers are widespread and used by many investment advisors. The major criticism of Elliott's analysis is that many traders feel the interpretation of the data is either highly subjective or that years of training are needed to be able to use the interpretation correctly

Some of the more common technical charts are bar charts, trend lines, channels, bar formations, continuation patterns, and gaps.

The risk of trading futures can be substantial. Margins are subject to change without notice. Minimum margins do not apply to spread positions. The highest degree of leverage that is often obtainable in futures trading due to small margin requirements can work against you as well as for you.